Old and Poor in 1970's New Orleans:

In Memory of Charles and Eva

CAB McLARTY

CreateSpace

Old and Poor in 1970's New Orleans:

In Memory of Charles and Eva

For information contact: Cab McLarty
e-mail: CabMcLarty@gmail.com

ISBN   978-1497542662

AUTHOR'S NOTE

I wish I could say that this is a work of fiction. Then it would be easier to deny that in our supposedly civilized country we would ever prey on the weak and helpless. And I wish that I could say this story is the product of a faulty memory of one who tends to recall the past through a glass darkly. Then it could be claimed that the account is biased and things were not as terrible as portrayed. And I wish I could say that this event only happened to one couple in one neighborhood. Then it could be said to be an aberration and not something to expect anywhere else.

Wishes, though, will not make it different than it was. This is based on a true story about the destruction of a neighborhood and the most helpless souls in it, a vignette of what it is like to be old and poor in a rapidly changing world. As such, it is a work of creative nonfiction. Conversations to which I was not privy are reconstructed to represent how the characters involved would have conversed. Of course, names and specific locations have been changed to protect the innocent as well as the guilty.

Also, this is not written from memory. It was originally put down on paper not long after the events occurred as a way of personally dealing with my anger at what had been done to people I cared about. It is being published now, as I grow old myself, as a way of giving some immortality to Charles and Eva and others like them who are nowhere else remembered.

Finally, this account is much larger than just a single New Orleans' neighborhood and one old couple in it. What is told here is the reality of life for many others in a variety of places, both then and continuing today.

Although this is a grim tale, within it is an uplifting lesson: even in the face of the worst adversity, laughter, love, and the joy of living is still about.

Without further ado, I give you Charles and Eva.

Old and Poor in 1970's New Orleans:

In Memory of Charles and Eva

Chapter 1

If you asked the bikini-clad lawyer's wife basking in the sun on the hood of her fifteen year old car how she knew Charles and Eva were coming home, she couldn't have told you. Neither could the preacher from next door who was hanging over their common fence ogling her. Old-man-Gaudet, slumped in his porch swing at the house across the street, might have known, but he never said. His mix of broken French and English was limited to ordering family members over to the corner store to buy him more whiskey and bananas. Most certainly Romeo knew because he always took off like a shot a few minutes before Charles and Eva showed up, but Romeo, the neighborhood stray cat, never talked either.

Something gave it away, floating in on the heavy New Orleans miasma to inform the neighborhood that the daily show was about to begin. One arm from the bikini-clad body moved over to turn down the country music blaring from her radio.   The preacher stopped his leering long enough to move back from the fence to a safer vantage point.   The Slovak woman from the opposite corner suddenly appeared on her porch and wedged her hulk into an ancient rocking chair.   Old-man-Gaudet found it the occasion to toss his banana peels on the sidewalk by Charles and Eva's door.   The Cranes, constantly scandalized at the goings-on in the neighborhood, expressed their opinion by slamming their front door and retiring into the only air conditioned apartment on the block.   Romeo and the half-blind feline soul-mate that he carried food to every day crept into their favorite vantage point under a large bush.   All eyes focused down Camp Street.

The first hint, more felt than heard, came as a distant pounding of a hammer rapping on steel.   The rod knocking in Charles' and Eva's ancient car engine had been protesting its lot far longer than anyone could remember, defying the predictions of all local, shade-tree mechanics and leaving the school-trained service boys at the Ford dealership scratching their heads in bewilderment.   Moments later, straining ears picked up the first hint of the roar from their unmufflered engine, followed by the syncopated crashing of one fender that persisted in flapping loosely back and forth.   Windows from which rubber stripping had long since melted rattled and a low moan came from air blowing over a hole in the windshield that had been caused by Eva's forehead in one of their numerous accidents.

Those listening expectantly could count the blocks as Charles and Eva neared.   Each stop sign was approached with disdain; nothing could stop these two.

At the last minute a twinge of conscience grasped at Charles, and he slammed on the brakes.   The tires squalled in protest, and the car jerked spasmodically from still being in gear.   Then came the sound of the engine roaring again as he slammed down the accelerator and with a vicious slipping of the clutch (for Charles hardly ever changed gears) rolled into the next nearer block.   This all took time, of course, because Charles and Eva rarely went over twenty miles per hour.

One block away from where the audience awaited them, the street curves slightly in order to follow the pattern established by the natural bending of the Mississippi River.   Around this turn they came, Charles shoved back in his seat with his arms out straight on either side of the steering wheel as if driving a sports car, Eva's face covered with a spider web created by the cracks in the broken windshield.   The headlights wavered erratically back and forth several times as the driver tried to decide how to aim at his destination.   Settling on a route at the last possible moment, he suddenly headed down the wrong side of the street, scraping along the curb, tires squalling in protest, until, jumping the curb, he ended up with one wheel on the sidewalk.   There was no lurching of the clutch, no grinding of gears, for Charles had killed the engine halfway down the block.   It was a moment of respite, the moment of silence when the curtains are rolled back on the stage and the audience waits with bated breath for the first lines in a production that has run so long every word of the script is known by heart.

"Gawd-dammit, gawd-dammit, gawd-dammit," Eva cursed as her door crashed open.   She had planted both her feet against it and given a vicious shove. "Gawd-dammit, gawd-dammit, gawd-dammit, Charles. Did you see that bitch?   Did you see what she did? Did you see that gawd-damned bitch trip me? Gawd-dammit, gaaaaawd-dam her.   Look at my leg! Just look at this bruise.   Look at it!   LOOK AT IT! That gawd-damned hussy.   I'll get ...."

   "Shush, Eva."   Charles tried to stop the tirade. "Just shush your mouth.   Can't you be quiet, just for a minute?" he pleaded.   "That woman didn't trip you on purpose.   You just can't see straight and ran over her foot.   Probably hurt her more than it did you.   You're just getting mean, old woman, with all your fighting at keno.   They're going to stop letting us play if you keep it up.   Always causing trouble.   Always!   God, I wish you'd act your age.   And what're the neighbors going to think?" he muttered, suddenly lowering his voice as he realized he, too, had been yelling into a silence that can only be created when all ears are straining to hear. He looked around for someone to apologize to for the scene they were making.   The nearest person, though, was only old-man-Gaudet, and he was looking straight ahead, slowly gumming a banana, acting as if oblivious to anything going on around.

   Charles didn't have time to apologize anyway before Eva started up again at the top of her lungs.   "You don't tell me what to do, Charles Pruitt.   I haven't put in ninety-two years on this earth just to have some old man telling me to shut up.   That gawd-dammed bitch hurt my leg, I'm telling ya.   Just look at it!   I'll get her ...."

   "Eva, SHUT UP," Charles suddenly yelled in exasperation,   heat   rushing   to   his   face   in embarrassment at the thought of what people must think of these two old fools yelling at each other.

"Eeyiii, eeyiii to you, Charles!" Eva yelled back at him.   Before he could open his mouth to hush her again, she stomped off down the sidewalk, stepping in perfect cadence with her continuing "eeyiii!   eeyiii! eeyiii!"   The neighbors observing had to restrain their impulse to applaud in admiration at the skill with which the two actors could bring down the curtain on their daily drama with such style and in such a consistent manner.

Charles trailed along behind, not knowing whether to look around and smile at the people casting furtive looks in his and Eva's direction or to walk with his head down in shame as he felt like doing.   His attention was diverted from either option as he suddenly realized that he was following Eva's exact path down the sidewalk and walking to the same cadence that she was setting with her continuing eeyiii's.   "Damn!" he muttered, in one of his rare expletives.   "Why in the world do I tag along behind following her exact path when she can't walk a straight line if she wants to?   If she would only wear her glasses in public, but she's so vain.   Blind as a bat without them."   The sobering thought that she might fall and hurt herself pushed him to hurry and catch up to her.   As slow as he was, he still managed to reach the steps to their apartment two paces ahead of Eva because she had missed seeing them and had to turn around and come back.   Like an angry kid, she jerked her arm away from his supportive grasp, but when he reached for it a second time, she didn't resist and let him steady her as she made it up the three steps.

Across the porch and into the alcove to their apartment door required three normal paces.   That would be six steps for Eva and, maybe, four for Charles. Pulling loose from Charles supporting hand, she crossed the space quickly, confidently, planting her heels firmly.   She neither saw the place where the rotten flooring had previously given way nor heard the ominous cracking of wood as her right foot came down on the hole's splintered edge.   Weeks back, she had given birth to the hole when her foot had buried to the ankle as they were returning from a keno game.   With no lingering memory of that and oblivious to the danger, she marched ahead, a proud woman.

Behind her, Charles watched the performance and addressed the sky.   "Lord, thank you for Eva's guardian angel.   If she didn't have one around here close, she'd be under the house by now."   Grasping the stair railing, he stepped on the first step and swung his stiff leg up behind him.   The railing swung out loosely under his weight as the screws holding it pulled a little further from the rotting wood, but it held as he completed his slow climb.   He worked his way around the hole Eva had just missed, knowing that it was just a matter of time until one or the other of them, or one of the other tenants in the building, fell through what was left of the floor.   I'll talk to McLaughlin one more time about fixing this, he thought, knowing even as he did that it would do no good.   Past attempts had shown that the landlord wasn't one to do much about taking care of problems.

By the time Charles caught up to her, Eva had spilled her purse by their front door and was threatening to start another tirade against purse makers, people who didn't light doorways, lock makers, and anyone else who was responsible for her not being able get her key out of the purse quickly.   Fortunately for Charles, but unfortunately for the neighbors who were still engrossed in this encore variation from the daily drama, the key was on top of the pile of lipstick, dirty kleenex, powder compact, glasses, hearing aid, and other assorted personal items that had littered the alcove.

The door wearily opened, following the circular path that it had long ago scraped in the linoleum under it.   The bright, Louisiana sun cut a dusty tunnel through the gloom and was absorbed by the dingy wallpaper on the opposite wall.   Charles unconsciously punched at the old-fashioned button light switch to the right of the door and just as quickly pulled his hand back.   Their electric bill was killing them, constantly going up, and making them have to scrape for the pennies to pay it.   The increases were due to a shortage of oil, claimed the city utility company, denying any responsibility, and the public would just have to conserve if they wanted to have lower costs.   In response, Charles and Eva had conserved, having agreed to leave the lights off as much as possible, and were now living most of the time in darkness.   The bills kept climbing anyway, now siphoning money away from their food budget. Funny, though, Charles thought, as he pulled his hand back and left the lights turned off, how I still have the habit of hitting at the switch when I enter a room.

Actually, there was another reason he didn't want any more illumination than necessary.   Once, when they had first moved in, he had opened the curtains, letting full light into the room.   The sight had so depressed him that they had not been opened since. Wallpaper that didn't look so bad in the gloom had suddenly shown the faded pattern of decades of wear. In one corner, the paper was gone where some former tenant had started burning it off with a blowtorch. The scorched remnants still stuck to the cracked plaster.   Golf ball-sized pieces of plaster that had fallen lined the baseboard, and the oak lathing showed through from a card table-sized hole in the ceiling. The chimney was gradually collapsing in upon itself, and the fireplace, in front of which the privileged of New Orleans had once sipped their brandy while watching the dancing flames reflect on the ornate mantle, was now gorged with bricks threatening to spew forth on the floor.   The mantle was long since gone.   Over all was the dust of generations: over the bed in the corner, the broken-down easy chair, the television and its orange-crate stand, the electric fan. It turned everything to the same hue.   It swirled when Charles and Eva moved, and it settled again when they settled.   A broom did nothing to remove it.   It only upset the dust that then got its revenge by making Eva wheeze and by grinding a little deeper into their skin after they had gone to bed.   Perhaps a vacuum cleaner would have sucked it up, but they didn't have one.   So, Charles thought, it's just as well to leave the lights off and the curtains drawn.

He settled heavily into their one over-stuffed chair, shifting his weight sideways to avoid a broken spring in the cushion.   Not too bad for two dollars at the St. Vincent de Paul Thrift Store, he thought, pleased at the memory of their recent good fortune at finding the chair.   Usually, the best they could hope for at the thrift shop was junk left over after the store's workers and volunteers had already picked through donations and taken any good items for themselves.

Eva, as quiet now as she had been loud a few minutes before, threw her coat and purse on the lumpy, brown bedspread.   Slowly, she began to undress and turned to look knowingly at Charles.

Later, when Charles awoke, Eva lay asleep beside him, a dark form illuminated by the street lamps forcing their light through tears in the curtains.   Who would ever think it of a ninety-two year old woman? Or a seventy-nine year old man, for that matter?   He laughed silently and affectionately patted Eva's bare bottom.   Taking her to keno is a real pain, he thought, what with her fighting and hell-raising.   And it takes me away from visiting with the neighbors in the evening.   But it's worth it, he smiled, because when she wins a nice pot at keno, there's always something special for me when we get home.   Sleep came again as he listened to the pigeons cooing softly to each other from their nests inside the walls of the decaying old house.

Chapter 2

Marc, before you climb down, finish that one little piece of trim that's left. Al will wait, won't you?" The slim woman in her paint-spattered, blue blouse and tan slacks playfully shoved at her cousin-in-law. Al Isaacs jerked away, cringing at the thought of Lori's grimy hands on his new suit.

"Come on. Finish it later," he answered, trying hard to keep the irritation out of his voice. "I've got to get back to the office." Damn, he grumbled to himself. You'd think all I've got to do is stand around watching these two painting on this old house. Never one to be patient, he shuffled from foot to foot.

"Ho, Roland! Looks like you've got the better job there." Halfway down the ladder Marc Isaacs spotted his next door neighbor and called over to him.

"That's what you think," Roland yelled back from where he was steadying a ladder while his wife painted high above. "I'm getting covered up with all the paint she's dropping. We've all got it easy, though, compared to them."   He pointed diagonally across the street.   "Look at those two hard at it."   All turned to see two people struggling onto their porch with a large, heavy mantle.

Anywhere they might have looked, they would have seen something similar going on.   The neighborhood was buzzing with people painting, scraping, sawing, and hammering.   It was Saturday, and it seemed that all the young professionals who had recently bought these run down houses for a song from their slum-lord owners were here.   They were proud to possess these new toys.   They smiled and worked and grilled steaks and drank wine and smiled some more.   On Monday morning they would be gone away to their jobs and the kids would be off to their private academies.   The real workers would show up to do the hard jobs and signs would sprout in the yards stating that the houses were being remodeled by some construction firm or another. But, on the next Friday evening, the signs would be pulled and the young owners would be back again to ogle and point at someone on a ladder.   They would get a spot of paint on their noses, smash a finger or two, laugh, smile, be happy, and, of course, brag about how hard they were working.   Quickly, they were changing the neighborhood from one that had originally held thousands in its paint peeling tenements to one filled with the fresh-faced houses suitable for holding a handful of young professionals and their scarce-few children.

"Come on, Marc.   Get down here, will you?"   Al couldn't keep the exasperation out of his voice.   "I really do have to get back.   I've got a luncheon appointment with the assistant district attorney at

12:30, and I need to talk to you and Lori first."

"That's always been your problem, Al," Marc chided his first cousin.   "You work too much.   Here it is Saturday.   You ought to be out of that office of yours. Out of these clothes."   He fingered the lapel of Al's suit coat.   "Buy yourself one of these places, Al, and you and Karen will start enjoying life more."

"Don't tell me how to live my life," Al snapped. "I'm doing all right.   And whose hard work is it, anyway, that's bankrolling this place for you?"   He motioned toward the house.   "Don't forget who loaned you the down payment."

"Take it easy, Al.   It was a joke, just a joke." Sometimes Marc didn't like his overly sensitive cousin very much at all.

"Apology accepted," Al muttered.   Mentally, he berated himself for throwing out that last comment about the loan, rubbing it in that he had done better financially than Marc and Lori.   It was dumb for him to risk alienating them right at the moment he badly needed their help.   "Actually," he went on aloud, "I need to tell you something.   In a way I hate to admit this after teasing you all about this place so much, but Karen and I are thinking of buying one ourselves. That's why I wanted to talk to you two."

"What?" Lori gasped.   "Don't joke with me like that.   We've wanted you to move near, wanting the kids to grow up with relatives close by.   But you've been so adamant that you wouldn't.   I don't believe it."

"Incredible.   It is incredible."   Marc shook his head in disbelief.   "After laughing at us for so long for what we're doing, now ....   Yeah, it's great, but I agree with Lori.   I'll believe it when I see it."

"Well, believe it." Al said. "It's going to happen if we can solve one problem that's holding us up, and that's what I want to talk to you about. There's a place I've got my eye on, but I'm having trouble getting it. I can use your help."

"You know we'll do whatever we can," Lori said. In her excitement she was ready to promise anything. She already was totally committed to getting people to buy and restore the dilapidated houses that had once been homes for the better class of New Orleanians. Parties and get-togethers found her working the room preaching with an evangelist's zeal the merits of preserving the city's history and increasing its property tax base. She, along with the others like her, were proud of what they were accomplishing and glad to bear the label "New Hope" that the city's administration used in promoting the movement. The fact that the two new converts, Al and Karen, were relatives only added to her excitement.

"Let's go into the house to talk," she said, her last words indecipherable. They were drowned out by the roar of an unmufflered engine from a derelict car that was rolling slowly down the street. One fender, about to fall off, banged loosely back and forth, adding to the cacophony of sounds emanating from the rolling wreck. Stares of resentment followed the noisy intruders.

"Well, it looks like things aren't quite so nice here after all." Seeing the looks of distaste on Lori's and Marc's faces, Al couldn't help but make the snide remark.

"Yeah, but they're temporary," Lori shot back. "You buy the house you're talking about and rebuild it, and others like you do the same, and problems like that will just go away.   Believe it.   They'll just go away."

Chapter 3

Charles' eyes skimmed the pile of make-up, old hose, razors, colognes, and trimmers that Eva had accumulated on her dresser. There were her glasses which she had needed when he first met her. Over the years they had evolved in thickness as she became blind in her right eye and lost vision in her left. Her hearing was also bad, a side effect of years of work in a noisy factory. But vanity had refused to let her wear a hearing aid until she was over sixty years old. Even now, at ninety-two, she would only put it on when it could be completely hidden. At age seventy, she had finally bought false teeth, but this came only after she had refused to smile in public for ten years. This concession was quickly followed by another as she began to wear wigs to cover the few wisps of red hair that were left. Charles couldn't help but chuckle at the thought of the many fights they'd had over items in Eva's pile of paraphernalia.

"What're you laughing at?" Eva yelled, the way she

always did with her hearing aid out.   Truthfully, she mostly yelled when she had it in, too.   "You're starting to talk to yourself like an old man," she said, playfully. "Now would you stop your staring and let me get ready for keno?"

Charles ambled back into the living room to wait. He was still smiling at the memories of the two of them when he plopped into his chair.

He couldn't remember when he had first met Eva; it had been so long ago.   He would never forget, though, where and how it had happened.   She had come to see her brother Frank at his fledgling insurance business, and the newly hired Charles had watched her stride across the floor toward the boss' office.

"She wasn't pretty, and looks weren't what caught my attention," he had recalled later to Frank.   "She was small and wiry with the craziest red hair I'd ever seen.   But there was something about the way she walked.   You would have thought she owned the world."

That was years before being an assertive or independent woman was considered a good thing. Eva was just known as cantankerous by most or "full of the devil" if you listened to her dad who had thrown her out of the house for not wanting to get married like her sister.   For the office workers on that day, Eva's spirit had provided a real treat.

"Gawd-dammit, gawd-dammit, Frank!"   Eva backed out of her brother's office, cursing as she came. The office-girl shrieked and clapped her hands over her ears to keep out such unladylike language.   "You're not going to tell me what to do, gawd-dammit!   I'll go to the Fairgrounds everyday if I want to.   And I'll bet any horse that I want to.   And I'll lose if I want to. It's my gawd-damned money.   I made it running that stinking sewing machine in that stinking pants factory for twenty stinking years, and I'll spend it any gawd-damned way I want."   Crash!   The door slammed behind her, the glass threatening to explode and the bell hanging from it to announce the entrance of customers breaking loose and flying across the room.

Later, after they had become close friends, Frank told Charles the whole story.   "Yes, Eva did work in a 'stinking' pants factory," Frank laughed at his sister's description, "for over twenty years and never got a promotion or anything during all that time.   To them, she was just another country girl come to town, willing to work for peanuts while she waited on getting married.   They didn't have to promote her because she needed the work to live and there were others lined up willing to take her job.   And I figure, too," he added, "that they didn't like her very much because she wouldn't take anything from anybody without letting them know about it.   Twenty years in a 'stinking' pants factory.   Yeah, that's a long time."   Frank just shook his head.   "I guess what aggravates me most about her, though," he continued after a minute, "is that she worked damned hard there and pinched every penny in order to save some.   Then, what does she do? Instead of investing that money wisely so she could live without having to work so hard, she blows it on the horses.   So, then the plant moves to Mexico, and there Eva is nearly fifty years old and without a cent to her name."

Even more years later, it was Eva who explained to

Charles how her gambling had come to be.   It had started, she told him, when, one day, she accidentally got onto the wrong streetcar and took a long detour out of her way.   She enjoyed the experience of riding through unexplored territory so much that by the time she got to her original destination she had decided to do it again, to start picking a streetcar at random and riding it wherever it was going.   At the end of the line she would get off to walk in strange neighborhoods, to eat, or to shop before returning to her rooming house. It would be the cheap entertainment that she had been looking for as a release from her mind-numbing job.

On one particular Saturday, the streetcar line she had chosen ended up at the Fairgrounds racetrack. There, for the first time in her life, she discovered a place where she felt truly at ease.   The atmosphere fit her personality perfectly.   She could ride the streetcar to the track with boisterous crowds whose gaiety she could enjoy without having to respond.   In the stands, she felt as one with others who had similar concerns and who could give a quick expression of sympathy when she lost without demanding more than that. She could stand in line, one anonymous entity among many others, and pay her money at the window, collecting a ticket from a stone-faced clerk who never showed approval or disapproval at her bets.   Later, she could collect from a similarly sober-faced person without ever divulging anything about herself.   It was exhilarating.   Such freedom she had never known.

The only problem for Eva was that she consistently picked losing horses.   She placed her bets on how she felt.   The worst-groomed horse looked good to her because she was sorry for it. The one handled harshly in the gate would draw her dollars as compensation for the cruelty of humans.   This woman who was so harsh and hard with other people was a sucker for the temperamental animal, the one difficult to control. And her hidden, soft-heartedness led to losses that by decade's end left her destitute.

"Charles, I don't know what I'm going to do about Eva," Frank said.   The two of them had just sat down for lunch at a sandwich shop on Poydras Street, close to the insurance office.   There had been some tough early years for Frank, but, in spite of them, the business had prospered.   Charles had become vice-president, and he and Frank were together often.   Over the years, Eva had more and more frequently joined their informal luncheons, but she was absent on this particular day, and she was the main topic of conversation.   "No matter what I say, Charles, Eva just won't stop her betting.   She's lost everything now, including what I gave her from the family estate five years ago.   I've told you before that our folks cut Eva out of their will. They never liked her ways.   But I was able to defer over to her some of what they left me so she could survive.   Now, she's gambled all that away, and if I give her more she'll just lose it.   So, what do I do?   I can give her just enough to live on, but, for chrissakes, I feel like a fool giving a fifty-five year old woman an allowance.   Besides," he continued," you know Eva. She's liable to kill us both when we suggest it."

    "What do you mean 'we'?" Charles interrupted. "This is your family affair, not my business."

    "Oh, but it will be," Frank said, laughing, "after I tell her it was your idea."

Charles never heard the details of what went on between Frank and Eva.   It had been, in fact, a family affair.   But he did learn that, as Frank had thought, she had been irate at the idea of an allowance.   She would either earn her own way or nothing at all, she had insisted.   And on the Monday following Charles' chat with Frank, she showed up at the insurance office. She would work for the older brother, earn her own money, and give up betting on the horses.

As the years went by, Eva spent more and more time in Charles' office.   She especially made it a point to show up on those mornings when he would drag in after a night of drinking.   He always made it to work. Perhaps he would have survived longer if he hadn't. But he would make it in, trying to inconspicuously steady himself on desks as he passed, his clothes rumpled from days of wear, and his eyes red and leaking from alcohol and lack of sleep.   Eva would bring him a welcome cup of coffee, sit down, and watch and listen.

"I don't fool anybody out there, you know?" he said to her, waving toward the outer office that he had just carefully negotiated.   "Just look at them when I come in.   I can't see an eyeball in the room.   They get so busy working."

Charles had never let his drinking interfere with his work.   Then, his wife died, and, suddenly, he just couldn't get enough of the stuff.   He often wondered why.   It wasn't from grieving over her as his friends thought.   It was true that he missed her.   Anyone would have who had lived with another for twenty-five years.   But he hadn't been madly in love with her, and they hadn't been particularly close.   "I know my drinking has hurt me here lately, Eva, but I'll be damned if I'll quit.   I drink because I want to.   I like it.   It's something I really enjoy, and that's the only reason that matters," he said emphatically.

"I know, Charles.   I know how it is, because that's why I still gamble.   Because I want to and enjoy it." Eva said it so quietly and matter-of-factly that it took a minute to register in Charles' fogged brain.   Suddenly, he understood and couldn't help but laugh aloud in spite of his splitting headache.   He wasn't the only one who had been keeping secrets from Frank.   "I still go to the track; I just sneak off now."   She continued her confession.   "I have changed a little, I guess.   I don't go as often as I used to, and I'm much more careful about my bets.   I win enough so that I'm not breaking myself, and I've started playing more bingo and keno because they're cheaper.   Frank thinks I'm getting religious going to bingo."   She laughed.   "But I still gamble; I just like it.   I just want to do it, and I'll be damned if I'll quit, either."   Their laughter sealed a permanent bond of friendship between them.

The difference between the two was that Eva worked successfully to keep her vices hidden from Frank.   Charles did not, and his binges affected his job performance more and more.   It seemed that his friendship with Eva strengthened in perfect parallel with the decline in his relationship with Frank.   Still, Charles never dreamed about how events would turn out for either Eva or himself.

"Why'd you do it, Charles?   Why'd you do it?" Frank demanded to know, pushing past the staggering

Charles and picking his way through the ruins of broken chairs, bottles, and leftover meals.   "Now, I've got to ..., I've got to ...."   He couldn't bring himself to finish.   "If you had just stayed at home, I could have lied like I've done many times and said you were sick. You could have gone away someplace.   I would have covered for you.   But you, but you had to come to the office and make an ass of yourself and of me."   Frank's voice took on a bitter edge of anger.   "Dammit, Charles.   Listen to me!" he suddenly shouted at the swaying, befuddled figure before him.   "You son-uv-a-butch.   Look at yourself.   You've pissed all over yourself, and you don't even care.   Drinking yourself to death in this pigsty."   Frank angrily flung his   arms   out   at   the   surrounding   destruction. "Dammit, Charles!"   Tears of frustration welled up in Frank's eyes.   "Think of the years.   Nearly thirty of them.   Thirty years we've been together.   Together, we've seen the business go from the bottom to the top. Now it all comes to this.   I would never have dreamed it would end like this."   Frank turned for the door. "Charles," he said, his voice mournful, but emphatic. "Don't come back to the office.   Not again.   Not ever. I'll have your check and your personal things sent out to you.   I don't want to see you again."   Frank slammed the door on his way out.

Charles hadn't said a word.   He was still trying to remember when he'd even been to the office.

The sound of the screen door slamming rapidly back and forth worked its way through the layers of fog that enveloped Charles.   As he had done for days when disturbed, he reached for the case of liquor beside him on the floor.   Eyes closed, his hand groped through the emptiness where full bottles had been.   The slamming of the door was louder and more persistent.   "Where's that damned bottle?" he muttered, as his eyes opened haltingly to see an empty box mutilated by his previous groping and soaked with the remains of a bottle spilled beside him.   "Oh, no!" he exclaimed, rolling over and pressing his face into the saturated carpet, inhaling the precious aroma.   Oh God, I need a drink, he thought, but that damned knocking.   It couldn't be somebody at the door.   God, no!   Just leave me the hell alone! But the pounding continued to drive through his tormented body until he was forced to make the long journey to see who it was.

Eva stared back at him through the torn screen. She had been trying to wake Charles by urgently opening and slamming the screen door.   "Charles," she started with the speech she had carefully prepared in order to explain her presence here.   She was going to tell him about resigning from her job and applying for retirement under Social Security, for which she had just become eligible.   She was going to omit the description of the major fight with Frank that her move had precipitated.   But she was totally unprepared for the wasted, filthy figure who suddenly stood in front of her.   Taken back, she hesitated, giving Charles a short respite for his aching head, as she collected herself. "Ah, the hell with it," she muttered to herself, pushing past him, dragging two suitcases with her.   "I'm going to take care of you," she declared.   Thus began their life together.

Chapter 4

Charles was napping soundly, a rare event for him, when an acrid stench wended its way into the room, set his nose to twitching, and yanked him awake. "What's that I smell?" he yelled toward the kitchen.

"Gawd-dammit, gawd-dammit, gawd-dammit!" Eva burst from the bedroom where she had been involved in her ritual of preparing for keno. "I've burnt the beans we were going to have for supper. Gawd-dammit, gawd-dammit! I can't remember anything anymore, can't do anything right." In spite of the cursing, Charles could tell she was close to tears.

"It's okay, Eva. It's okay," he yelled as he hobbled after her into the kitchen. It's amazing that she remembers as well as she does, he thought. After all, she is ninety two. But it was also true that she was forgetting more and more, and when she did, she would get so depressed that she was just ready to give up living. Somehow, he had to keep that from happening. He loved her and depended on her.

They needed each other, and he had to think of something to make her feel better.

"Eva!" he yelled again to get her attention.   He need not have bothered, because the crisis had already passed.   She was focused on the smoke-belching pot that she was holding at arm's length.   He smiled in relief as he watched her drop it into the sink where it sent up a plume of steam from its dying heat.   She had always been such a perfectionist, such a proud person. How long, Charles wondered, would he be able to continue diverting her attention away from the fact that her days of perfection were gone forever?

A while later, Eva walked into the living room where Charles was sitting.   "How do I look?" she asked.

Oh, my God! Charles nearly let the exclamation slip.   He'd forgotten that she was going to wear her new dress tonight, and, when she wore something new, she made such a big deal out of it with the neighbors that it embarrassed him to death.   "You look great, Eva," Charles said.   "Really great."   Even as he spoke he knew that none of Eva's clothes looked good on her. She rarely had the money to buy new ones.   When she did, they were from bargain basements and discount stores.   But even expensive clothes are not made for people like Eva and probably would have looked little better.   At ninety-two years of age, she had shrunk to skin and bones.   Breasts that had never developed fully and that had never been helped by birthing were like prunes, filling out nothing.   So her dresses were more akin to sacks than well-fitting outfits.   She tried hard to dress up, though, and Charles always lied when she did.   "That dress is sure pretty on you," he added.

"It's her pride that keeps her going."   Charles had explained to Steve, the upstairs tenant with whom he was particularly close.   "It's what helps her put up with age and everything that goes with it.   As long as I can help her keep it, I will.   Course," he laughed, "there've been plenty of times when it has caused trouble, too.   Then, I've sure wished she had a little less of it."

Steve, and anyone else who ever saw Eva walk, didn't have to be told that she was a proud woman. Head erect, shoulders back, she planted her heels firmly into the sidewalk and hammered her slight body down onto her frail legs.   With no body fat left to absorb it, the shock from this maneuver would drive through and vibrate her entire frame.   One day, in full view of the evening crowd of sidewalk-standers and porch step-sitters, it shook her wig completely off her head and onto the sidewalk.   No one laughed.   There wasn't a sound as everyone waited to see what Eva would do.   To their amazement, she walked on, oblivious to her loss.   Dinner tables, though, resounded with laughter that night as the tale was told about the old lady and her wig.   "God, she looked funny," was repeated over and over, "with her head covered with pins and wisps of red hair sticking up all over, swaying as she walked."

The neighbors didn't want to embarrass Eva by letting her know they had seen her wigless.   So, after a brief discussion among themselves, they decided to say nothing but just place it outside her door.   The following day, it was gone without a word.

A few weeks later, it was Eva's hearing aid that was jarred from her ear and lost.   For several days afterward, Charles' and Eva's apartment walls were thinner.   Their lovemaking became community entertainment as Eva enjoyed talking during sex, and this she now did in full voice.   The straight-laced Cranes from next door, appalled at the sounds that emanated from the house, chose to stay indoors even more that they usually did.   As for the other tenants, they smiled and nodded knowingly when passing Charles and Eva.   Charles returned the smiles and nods, thinking that everyone was certainly friendly, until he began to catch on to what they were all about. Then, the fight that followed was further enjoyed by the neighbors.   "You damned old woman with all your grunting and groaning," Charles yelled.   "Why can't you be quieter?   Everybody around here is laughing at us."

Eventually, the hearing aid was found and returned, but, just as the neighborhood got back to a much less exciting normal, Eva lost her glasses. Charles endured several days of anxiety as she wandered about refusing assistance from anyone. There were occasional crashes from inside the apartment, and she had to be rescued once from an azalea bush into which she had walked.   The entire tenement house smelled from the food she was scorching because she was unable to see if the stove was on or not.   Finally, after the Social Security checks came in, she was able to buy another pair of glasses, and the crisis was over.

By this time, the neighborhood was really into the saga of Eva and her paraphernalia.   Bets were laid and lost on when and what she would lose next.   Even with all the interest, however, no one could possibly have guessed what it would be.   To this day, it is still uncertain as to how she lost them for no one saw it happen, and Eva certainly wouldn't tell.   In fact, she consistently denied that it happened at all.   Somehow it did, because, when Steve was walking home from the bus stop one afternoon, there in front of him on the sidewalk were Eva's teeth, both plates, uppers and lowers.   At least, he assumed they were Eva's teeth. No one else went around losing essential body parts.

Deep in thought about other problems, he didn't really consider how to approach Eva with her teeth nor did he dream there would be a problem with getting her to take them back.   Before climbing the stairs to his own place, he simply knocked at Charles' and Eva's door to return them.   Eva answered, obviously upset that Charles was asleep and that she had to be seen without looking her best.   Barefooted, wigless, in a slip that hung loosely from her shoulders, she spied what Steve had in his hand and started talking before he had time to say a word.

"Those aren't my teeth!" she slurred loudly through lips flapping from the lack of support behind them. "Don't bring those things in here, because I don't have false teeth."   When she stopped talking, her lips receded into the space between her gums.   Wrinkles formed around her mouth pointing accusingly at the cavity where her teeth normally rode.

Surprised by her indignation, Steve backed away and motioned toward the floor.   "I'll just leave them here by the door, then.   You can get them later."   He didn't know what else to do, but he did know that she needed them and didn't have the money to buy another pair.

"Don't you leave those there," Eva ordered. "They're not mine, I tell you.   Don't leave them."   She slammed the door.

The next day the teeth were still there.   Steve told Charles the story, and he took them to give to her after she had settled down.   But Eva's mouth remained the same.   She never wore the teeth again.   "Like I've told you before," Charles explained to his perplexed neighbor, "Eva is a proud woman."

Chapter 5

Heading west away from downtown New Orleans and the French Quarter, a driver will find that every few blocks he has to turn slightly right to keep from angling across the street and striking cars parked on the left side. Without these occasional bends, the streets would refuse to follow the natural curve of the Mississippi River and would eventually run into it. Each curve is slight, just enough to keep a driver alert for the next one, and they may almost go unnoticed by the stranger. But, to those who live here, the bends are more than just obstacles to negotiate while driving. They mark the progress of a war between two opposing ways of life. It is a deadly battle between those who have loved, lived, and died here and an invading force expanding outward, bend by bend, from Audubon Park and St. Charles Avenue, scorching the earth as it takes block after block, sucking all vestiges of human life from the neighborhoods it consumes.

A block away from Charles' and Eva's place there

was a bend in Camp Street that marked the nearest advance of the enemy.   On the older couple's side of the line were people like themselves.   On the other side was the New Hope, as they were being called by city officials, and a less formidable-looking invasion force would be hard to find.   They seemed to always be smiling, especially when conversing with others of their own kind, and they were all so terribly homogenized it was hard to tell them apart.   They were the same age, uniformed   similarly,   hair   styled   alike,   with interchangeable, cloned kids.   You could drive through the New Hope blocks and see the doors gaping and windows staring vacantly as people busily scraped and painted their newly captured houses.   With their children watching from the shade where they were being corralled by nannies, women and men swiped at windows, pushed a broom across a porch, but mostly stood in the yard and pointed up at someone else on the ever-present ladder.   They all scurried busily around as if working so hard, yet their hands were rarely dirty.   Eventually, the day would come when the contractors and their employees, the only ones around not playing at their labor, would pull their remodeling signs out of the yards and leave.   Then the New Hope would proudly enter their beautifully refurbished houses to rarely come out again.   Another block once warm and vibrant with human beings would now be as cold and empty as the souls of the invaders.   Another neighborhood improved, the New Hope would think, feeling good about their victory.   Now, it's time to invade another.

The New Hope loved what they were doing, spending their young professionals' salaries to restore the city.   They were preserving history, rebuilding what had been decaying, and they felt good about it. The city liked it, because the restored houses could be taxed at a much higher rate than the tenements being replaced.   All concerned in these efforts refused to note that each New Hope couple was taking over what had been the homes for four or more families.   None cared that the low rent area of the city was shrinking and that refugees displaced by the invasion were having to compete for a decreasing number of places to live. There were no feelings of guilt because conditions were worsening for the Charles and Evas of the city as slum rents inflated and took greater proportions of already too-small checks.   In a tradition as ancient as man himself, to the victor goes the spoils, and the New Hope took them without remorse.   Their advance was to the bend just beyond Charles' and Eva's and their plans for invading the next block were already laid.

Charles glanced at his alarm clock when he heard the low murmur of voices outside his window.   It was 10:30.   A Wednesday morning.   He and Eva had played keno until midnight, and that, combined with his usual nighttime restlessness, made him want to be left alone.   The lump on his left side ached, and he had slept with his hand gouged into it for relief.   As a result, his muscles had never relaxed, and he felt old, really old, like maybe eighty, he thought, grinning wryly at his little joke.   But who's that outside? he wondered.   It's not Mike or Steve or any of the other close neighbors.   They would have come to the door by now.   And as far as that bunch from around the bend. They wouldn't dare walk in this neighborhood

Charles was mostly right.   The New Hope did stay on their side of the battle line.   There were a couple of exceptions like the old Slovak woman who lived in the first house around the bend.   Somehow, years before, she had managed to buy her place and gain some security from being run out by a landlord.   No one held it against her, though, that she was a property owner because her house was as old and rotten as the rest around.

She was a character, not to be forgotten, which meant she fit into the neighborhood well.   She was famous for starting every conversation, regardless of its intent, with the heavily-accented shout: "I am a Slovak!   Not a dirty Czech."   Standing five feet ten inches tall and weighing in at over two hundred pounds, in her full-skirted peasant dresses and old-fashioned cotton stockings rolled down to bunch up around her ankles above black, lace-up, work shoes, she looked enormous.   When, with clenched fists on her adequate hips, she glared down from the heights of her porch and shouted her proclamation, real estate agents—the vanguard of the New Hope—would quickly decide it really wasn't worth asking her if she wanted to sell.   Neighbors knew she meant nothing by it.   It was much like others saying hello.

Rumor had it that when her old car was stolen, she was so beside herself that the cops could get nothing from her.   She kept asking over and over how someone could have done that to her.   "I'm a Slovak! To a Czech, yes.   But never to me.   How could they?" The police finally gave up trying to get information from her and didn't process the case.   As luck would have it, a few days later they found the car anyway, minus its engine. It was hauled back to sit rusting away beside her house, a thorn in the side of the New Hope and a constant reminder to them of the kind of people remaining to be conquered.

The only other person from around the bend who ventured into the neighborhood was a well-known TV newswoman who would get so drunk she didn't know where she was. Her well-groomed poodle, more interested in fun than snobbery, would drag her into the block on the end of its leash. She was always friendly when she encountered Charles or Eva or old-man-Guadet, and she was interesting to talk to when she could be understood. The voice outside was not hers, though, because she only got smashing drunk on weekends when she was not reporting the news.

So it wasn't the newswoman. It also wasn't the Slovak, Charles knew, because she would have paused to say good morning to old-man-Gaudet, and he would have heard them talking. His curiosity getting the better of him, he pulled himself slowly from bed and hobbled toward the door. The bell rang just as he got there.

The strikingly beautiful lady, trying to focus on Charles through the dirty screen of the door, was dressed simply, yet expensively. There was no doubt that she was a foreigner to this neighborhood, and Charles' first thought was that just once he wished Eva would have the money to buy a dress like the one this woman was wearing.

"Mr. Pruitt," the woman affirmed, glancing at her notepad, "I am Lori Isaacs from down the street." She nodded her head in the direction of the New Hope. "And this is Mrs. Fontenot." She indicated her companion.   "How are you and Mrs. Pruitt today?"

"Fine, fine," Charles answered reflexively, waiting for the woman to get to the point.   Bill collectors and Jehovah's Witnesses came by often, and he understood them.   This woman's being here was confusing, and his guard was up.

"Mr. Pruitt," she proceeded, "I bet there are things in this neighborhood you would like to see improved, aren't there?   I mean, it's not safe for any of us on the streets at night.   No one pays any attention to our problems, and the owners just let their places run down.   Now, that's not right, is it Mr. Pruitt?   And you would like to see those things changed, wouldn't you?   And Mrs. Pruitt, too," she glanced again at her pad, "would like to see things better, wouldn't she?   Well, a group of friends and I have gotten together for the purpose of trying to make our neighborhood a better place to live, and we've formed the Camp Street Improvement Association.   The first thing that the association is doing is talking to everyone in the neighborhood to see what problems there are that we need to work on.   Now, Mrs. Fontenot and I just noticed in passing by that your porch needs some work done on it, and we said to ourselves, 'We bet those people have tried and tried to get the owner to fix that, and he has refused to help them out at all.'   Now that's not right, is it, Mr. Pruitt?   You could get hurt badly, and where would the landlord be while you are in the hospital?   For sure, you know he wouldn't be there to help you.   Now, how long have you been trying to get him to fix this porch, Mr. Pruitt?"

As a former insurance man who had seen sales pitches made by the very best, Charles had to admire the woman's line.   She could have been selling flesh as a curbside hooker or dresses in a fashionable boutique. The approach was the same, and, in spite of himself, Charles' first thought was to wonder what she had sold to get to her present station in life.   He instantly felt a twinge of guilt at doubting her motives.   Maybe she really was concerned, he thought.   Her stance, her voice, the way she wrinkled her well-made-up brow made it seem so.   And if she were from around the bend, that meant she had connections that could make a difference.   After all, she was right in guessing that the landlord, McLaughlin, had paid no attention to Charles and never came around to see what was needed.   Here she stood, on the other hand, asking him for his opinion, asking him to complain, asking him if he had problems.   What would it hurt if he talked to her?   It was too good an opportunity to refuse, and, instead of slamming the door in her face as he did with other door-to-door sales people, Charles bought her concern and invited the two women in.

A few minutes later the two women backed out the door, Lori Isaacs still talking nonstop.   Angrily, she shook her pad and fumed.   "I cannot understand why anyone would ignore these kinds of things.   It's unthinkable, unforgivable, to let your place get like this.   The smell of leaking gas is so strong I don't know how you can stand it, and this hole in the porch," she stepped gingerly around its jagged edges, "is going to break a hip or something.   And that water dripping down your wall from the upstairs apartment, I hate to think of it, but that may be from their commode."   She visibly shuddered at the thought.   "How long did you say that has been running down there?" she asked and scribbled his answer as further ammunition on her pad.

"This is awful, just awful."   She was shaking that pad again. "I promise you, Mr. Pruitt, that we're going to get something done about this.   The Camp Street Improvement Association will take action on this immediately, and we're going to help you out.   This is despicable, making you live like this."   She was down the steps now and turned back to him.   "You've been a tremendous help, Mr. Pruitt, and we appreciate it. The neighborhood appreciates it.   Goodbye, now."

Charles smiled and with a final wave watched the two women make their way back in the direction of the New Hope.   It didn't dawn on him at the time to wonder why they didn't continue on to other houses on the block.   It was a point that would come back to him later.

"Who was that, Charles?" Eva yelled from the back room where she had been sleeping.   "That sounded like a woman.   Was that a woman, Charles? Gawd-dammit, Charles, I don't want any strange woman in this house.   Do you hear me, Charles? Gawd-dammit, I don't want any whoring women in this house.   Damn women!   Damn men!" she muttered, but Charles wasn't paying any attention to her.   He felt good, thinking about what had just occurred. Someone had listened to him and heard his complaints. Something good was going to come from this.   He felt it in his bones.

Chapter 6

The ambulance cut its siren off a block away and came in silent and menacing, gliding to the curb and releasing its uniformed occupants in a choreographed entrance. A few feet away, Charles stopped sweeping and rested on his broom, watching. He had been cleaning up glass from where someone had broken out a window of his car the night before. While sweeping, he had also been talking to a neighbor, the topic of conversation being Charles' son, Charles Jr., better known as Chuck. The neighbor took the ambulance's interruption as an opportunity to escape from the conversation as he had been at a loss for words as to what to say to a seventy-nine year old in poor health whose only son wouldn't bother to drive across town to see him.

Neither of the two men had to guess why the ambulance was here. Old-man-Gaudet had probably passed away. He had already been dead to them for weeks, and they had known it was only a matter of time until his body would follow.

Months before, first one and then others had begun to talk among themselves about how the neighborhood fixture, ensconced on his front porch, seemed gradually to be getting more and more feeble.   First noticed was that his daily treks to the liquor store were less frequent and that he was increasingly hitting up neighbors to buy his booze for him.

"Why not buy a fifth instead of a sack of half-pints?" hc was asked by one person agreeing to take his order.

"Nope, the little ones.   Get the little ones.   The others are too hard to hold."   He motioned with his arthritic hands.

On what was to be his own last trip to the liquor store, old-man-Gaudet had made his usual stop at the Salvation Army donation box located in the parking lot of a nearby supermarket.   He always liked to push open the flap covering the box's window and peer around inside to see what had been added in the last twenty-four hours.   This time, something in a back corner looked interesting, and he decided to pull it out to check on it.   But no matter how hard he reached and stretched and jabbed with his cane, he couldn't quite get a grasp on the pair of shiny, nearly-new boots that beckoned to him.   Brooding over his near good fortune, he ambled on.   Suddenly, he had an inspiration.   On his way home, he would stop back by, borrow one of the shopping carts from the grocery store, and get the extra reach he needed by standing up on it.

It wasn't a great idea, he discovered when his feeble body nearly refused to let him raise his foot high enough to get on the cart, but it was a good enough idea because it worked.   Teetering precariously on the bottom shelf of the cart, he stretched into the box and a second later had the boots in his hands.   He touched them, feeling the smoothness of their glossy tops contrasting with the coarseness of their new strings. Just a little pull, he thought, and they'll come free of whatever seems to be holding them.   Already, he could see himself sitting on the porch, eating his bananas, looking at himself in the shine on the beautiful boots, and listening to the admiring comments of the neighbors.

Without warning, he was suddenly inside the box. The basket had rolled away, tipping him over the opening's sill and somersaulting him into the pile of clothes and discarded goods below.   He was so shocked that he didn't hear the window, spring-loaded to hold it against wind and rain, as it slammed shut. It was several seconds before he realized he was trapped inside a Salvation Army box.

Fortunately--or unfortunately, given the events that followed--an attendant at a nearby gas station had been watching the episode unfold and came to the rescue. Aching from laughter at the ridiculous image Gaudet posed, he and several passersby pulled the old man through the window.   Gaudet slid out muttering darkly about donation boxes without handles on the inside and about young people who would laugh at an old man's plight.   But, as he wandered away toward his own place, he had his sack of half-pints in one hand and the boots clutched tightly in the other along with his cane.

Old-man-Gaudet told no one in the neighborhood

about the boot incident, and there would have been no long term effects if it had not been for the next morning's newspaper.   There on the front page of The Times-Picayune, the incident was recorded for all to see.   Unknown to anyone, there had been a reporter at the gas station, and she had captured the event frame-by-frame.   There was old-man-Gaudet standing on the grocery cart and leaning into the box.   Next, there was a picture of the box alone with the shopping cart a few feet away.   Then, there was a shot of Gaudet's head and arm protruding from the window. Last of all, there he was ambling away with the boots in hand.   The pictures had been used by the paper to illustrate the seriousness of poverty and the aged in New Orleans.

Old-man-Gaudet was devastated.   He wasn't poor, he declared.   He had his family, his liquor, and his bananas.   What else did he need?   And he might be old, but he sure as hell wasn't aged.   To be called those things was too much for him, and the humiliation was too great.   He never walked to the liquor store again, and he became increasingly feeble.   The few words he spoke became even more unintelligible.   He stopped gumming his bananas and for days sat slumped in the swing with his hat down, a half-pint clutched in his hand.   Everyone knew it was only a matter of time until it came, but the manner in which it occurred surprised them all.

Drop a box down a flight of steps or let a kid throw a toy down and hardly a head will turn.   No sense is alerted to sound an alarm.   But let a human fall down those same steps, and, instantly, everyone will be running to the scene.   Even without a cry from the one falling, there is something that screams out that this is a person, a body, a living human, tumbling head over heels, arms askew, head bouncing, out of control on this unnatural structure called steps.   Such sensitivity to others falling seems to be even more developed in the aged, a response, perhaps, to losing so many of their own in this way.   From wherever it comes, the oldest tenants, Charles and Eva, were the first to hear the dreadful sounds from the apartment next door.   A loud thud, a scraping on the wall separating the stairs from their apartment, then a slow repeating of the sounds that seemed to last forever as Gaudet slowly tumbled to the bottom.   There was silence.   Then came the expected screams and the sound of running feet.

Like the good extended Cajun family they were, Gaudet's daughter, her husband, Mike, and their children took care of the old man as best they could after the fall.   But he never regained consciousness and, for all purposes, was dead already.   It was only left for his body to follow.   Now it had.

There were too many people about on the street for the attendants to just grab the body and run.   By the time they carried the corpse out the door with the sobbing family trailing behind, a crowd of neighbors had gathered.   They shuffled about on the sidewalk talking in low voices about how they would miss the old man's banana peels and liquor bottles.   A few went up to offer comfort to one or another of the family who stood on the front porch watching the sheet draped stretcher slide into the van.

It was a somber crowd, generally quiet, except for the young lawyer who, his prematurely old face puffy with drink, wandered across the street from his place. Latching onto the straight-laced Mr. Crane, the first person he came to, he hoped loudly that the family didn't get one of those caskets made in Kentucky. "Why, I've got a case right now where the body broke through the bottom of one of them," he said.   "Rolled out in the floor in the middle of the funeral!   Right in front of the family.   What a mess.   But the family's going to make a mint with their lawsuit."   The lawyer laughed drunkenly at the ludicrous scene he had painted.   No one else joined in, and several looked as if they were ready to punch his face.   Charles stood apart from the crowd as he had done the entire time.

On Friday, Gaudet's body was hauled away.   On Saturday morning, Charles and Eva started out as usual on their drive down to Swendemans on Magazine Street to buy groceries.   Their old car always knocked, banged, and rattled as if it were going to quit at any moment, but, on this day, it seemed to threaten more than usual, with a new screeching sound added to the normal racket.   "We might have made it on to the store and back, but I was afraid that the car would quit on us in the middle of the street," Charles told Steve the story.   "And Eva and me, we couldn't have moved it. We have a hard enough time pushing a fork across a plate much less a car out of the street.   The thought of having to pay a tow truck scared us to death, so I pulled in that big service station there on the corner of Washington and St. Charles."

The manager was nice enough and reassured Charles and Eva, telling them that the problem was more than likely a small one.   He apologized for not being able to get to the car immediately but promised that he would look at it later that afternoon if they would leave it with him. The cab fare to get home worried Charles and Eva, but neither one of them could climb the steps on the public buses, and they didn't want to wait in the service station as there were several tough-looking punks hanging around. Deciding to go on home, they called the cab, paying the fare from their grocery money.

When Charles called later in the day to find out about the car, much to his surprise he was told that the manager had left for the weekend without looking at it. The boy who answered the phone said that he would check on it, and Charles could call back on Sunday. When Charles said that he needed the car sooner, the kid turned belligerent.

"He called me an old timer," Charles continued the story to Steve, "and that makes me mad as a wet hen when some young'un calls me that. But what were Eva and I to do? So, I told him that we would check tomorrow. So there we were with no car and Eva hollering that she wanted to go to keno. There was no food in the house, but I didn't want to bother anybody, so that's why I didn't ask you or Mike to go to the store for me."

On Sunday morning, Charles tried to call the service station. Getting no answer, he began to be very uneasy about the situation and decided to go get the car, fixed or not. It cost him taxi fare there and back to discover that the station was closed for business on Sundays and that his car was locked up inside where he couldn't get to it.

Charles was waiting when the station opened on

Monday morning.   "Oh, the manager's not here," the young fellow he had talked to on Saturday told him. "He doesn't come in on Mondays, but, I'll tell you what. I'll fix your car for you for three hundred and fifty dollars."

"The whole car's not worth that," Charles explained to Steve.   "So I told him I didn't have the money, that I would just have to take the car on with me.   Well, when I said that, the fellow started getting real smart, and his punk friends that were hanging around there started gathering around close, laughing and talking among themselves about 'this stingy old fart.'   I hate to admit it, but the truth is I started getting scared.

"Finally, he says I can take the car but I've got to pay a storage fee that's due on it.   It's been taking up their space, he says, and I owe them for that.   One hundred and fifty dollars he wants right there, cash only.   And he laughs at me when he says it, looking around at his hoodlum friends to make sure they're enjoying his little joke.   'Just for you, old man,' he adds, laughing, 'I'll knock off ten dollars and let you have the car back for one forty.'

"What could I do, Steve?   I couldn't tangle with those young bucks.   I tried to talk to them.   I tried to tell them that Eva and I had to have the car to get around.   But they just laughed at me.   'If it's that important to you, old timer,' he said, 'you'll get us the money.'

"So, what could I do?   I can't tell the police. Those punks know where I live, and they said they'd come and get me.   If I was young, I would take care of it.   But Eva and me, we can't live with somebody out to get us all the time.   So, I lost the car.   I had to leave it and walk away."

The day after telling Steve the story about losing their car, Charles was gone. Where he was off to or when he would be back, Eva wouldn't say, but, when neighbors asked about his whereabouts, she was adamant in her claim that he wasn't around. If what she said was true, though, she was certainly talking to herself more than usual, because the people in the apartments connecting with hers could hear the sound of muffled words through the walls. "Charles, honey, do you have to have that?" Eva's question could be made out distinctly. "But not too much more, now." She was heard to gently admonish someone.

The ambulance didn't glide in silently on this trip. It split the neighborhood with a vengeance, screaming its curdling tale, overpowering even the lawyer's wife's country music. The siren was still moaning when Eva rushed from the house. "Oh God! Oh God! Oh God! Oh God! Oh God! Please help me! Help me!" she screamed. "Poor Charles has killed hisself! He's killed hisself! Oh Charles! Oh Charles! Oh Charles! Please help him," she pleaded to the paramedics who had already rushed past her, jumping the hole in the porch as they ran.

No more than a couple of minutes later one of the young attendants came back out of the house and unhurriedly moved toward the ambulance. "When I decided to become a paramedic," she paused beside a couple of neighbors, "I never dreamed I would be wasting most of my time on drunks. By law, we've got to take care of him and take him in to the hospital, but it's just not right.   Someone might really need us, but we're stuck here with this old man who wants to drink himself into the grave.   Somebody could die because of this."   She stomped over to the ambulance to get some equipment needed for transporting Charles. The neighbors listening glared after her, her talking about their friend like she was not setting well with them.

Charles exited the house strapped to a stretcher but uncovered and very much alive.   Although holding his side and obviously in pain, he was lucid and attempted to smile at the neighbors who followed the paramedics' path to the ambulance.   "Steve," he whispered as he passed, "call my boy and tell him.   Call Chuck for me. Please."   Those were his last words as the attendants slid him into the ambulance.

Three days later Charles was home again.   Walking. All smiles.   He got out of the taxi and made his way up the walk as jauntily as one can at age seventy-nine and with a bum leg.   "Well, I fooled them again, Steve," he greeted his neighbor.   His voice was light, and he seemed in better spirits than he had been since well before Gaudet's passing and the loss of his and Eva's car.   "That young VA doctor has told me three times now that I'm going to kill myself if I drink again.   He told me that this time, and the last, and the time before that, too.   Well, I'm still here, aren't I?   Am I walking?   Do you see me right now?   I showed 'em, I did!   Why, I've got a lump.   Here, let me show you." He yanked out his shirt and exhibited a massive knot on his abdomen.   "The doc said this lump was caused from drinking, and it would kill me before my time if I didn't stop.   Before my time!   Can you believe that a doctor would try to threaten someone as old as me with something like that?"   Charles burst out laughing. Others gathered around him by the porch steps joined in while Eva stood in their apartment door smiling toothlessly, happy to have her Charles home again.

Gradually, the laughter quieted.   "I called Chuck like you asked," Steve said.   "Did he come to see you in the hospital?"

Silence fell over them, and Steve immediately knew he had brought up the wrong subject.   The answer to his question was written on Charles' face.

Chapter 7

The occupants of the strange car that was circling the block had come at the wrong time if they wanted to be invisible. It was right before dark when the color has just disappeared from the earth, when there is no hint of a breeze, and when in hot areas of the world everywhere people are sitting outside enjoying each other's company. In this particular block on Camp Street in New Orleans, the steps and porches were clogged with tenants. The Cranes, alone, remained by themselves on their little lawn, a patch so small that with their chairs on it, they had to rest their feet on the sidewalk. The preacher from across the street, as usual, was hanging over the fence ogling the lawyer's wife who, as predictably as rain on a New Orleans' summer afternoon, was flaunting what she had for him to see. Romeo, the cat, was wandering from step to step picking up pieces of attention where he could while his blind feline soul-mate followed closely behind.

On the second time around the block the dark-colored auto pulled to the curb, and the engine died.   A middle-aged gentleman stepped out and tried to appear nonchalant as he looked around.   His act didn't hide his discomfort at being in this neighborhood and at being stared at by at least twenty-five people watching his every move.   He refused to meet any of their eyes.

Of all people to have done so, it was the mostly blind Eva who first recognized the stranger and broke the ice.   "Charles!" she exclaimed, clutching Charles arm.   "That's Chuck!   He's here.   He's come to see you," she slurred happily, pointing at the approaching figure.

Charles pulled himself to his feet far faster than normal and stared hard at the approaching figure. He's older than he should be, Charles thought.   He's almost as gray as I am.   But how long has it been? Three, four years?   No, wait!   It was eight ....   Oh my God, it's been twelve years since I've seen him. Charles hobbled toward his son, wishing the years were returned to him.   He didn't want just eight, ten, or twelve.   He wanted all of them, all the way back to Chuck's birth.   Maybe, then, he could do it over again, do it right, and he and Chuck wouldn't be meeting this way.   They came together on the sidewalk and shook hands as strangers.

"How are you, Dad?" Chuck said.   "I'm sorry I couldn't get over to the hospital, but are you alright now?"

Eva had gotten over her initial surprise and was chattering away to everyone around.   "Oh, Chuck is a fine boy, a fine boy," she said.   "It's awful how he hasn't come to see Charles, but you can see he really is a fine boy, because he has come now.   It's not his fault, anyway, that he hasn't been over.   It's that gawd-dammed hussy he lives with that's no good.   That gawd-dammed hussy.   I know he'd come more often if it wasn't for her."

"Shush, Eva," totally unlike himself, Mike snapped at his next door neighbor.   He didn't want her to embarrass herself more, because he had just spied the hussy getting out of the car.

Chuck's wife dethroned in a perfectly choreographed performance for the watching audience. Swiveling in her seat, she very deliberately placed each foot on the ground and levitated slowly from the automobile.   She floated down the sidewalk, no striding or bouncing in her motion.   Such movement could not be allowed because her elaborate hairdo would never have sustained the shock.   Ghostlike in the twilight in a white suit, she halted momentarily to extract from somewhere within its folds a color-coordinated poodle that she then cuddled between her breasts.   The dog surveyed those around with the same distaste in its beady eyes as that reflected in its owner's.   "Charles, my dear," she said, offering him the tips of her fingers, "how are you?   You look so well."   Most listening couldn't help but smile at the lie.   Charles always looked like hell.

That was the end of the show for the neighborhood as Charles, Eva, the son, and daughter-in-law went inside to visit.   Later, Chuck's wife came out to let her poodle go to the bathroom.   Steve and Mike were still on the steps, and it made it difficult for her to pass without saying a little something.   "We would have driven our good car," she said, "but we were afraid to in this neighborhood.   That's why we drove that one." She inclined her head toward the one they had come in, one far better than any other parked in sight.   With a nervous titter, she returned to the apartment, leaving Steve and Mike silently looking at each other and shaking their heads.

A dark-green sedan, its engine dead, slowly rolled through the gutter in front of the house, bumped over the curb, and stopped with one wheel on the sidewalk. Who's this stopping in Charles' and Eva's parking spot? Steve wondered, looking up from where he'd been working on his own car.   Then, through the unbroken, clean glass of this strange automobile, Steve saw something he had never been able to see before through Charles' and Eva's windshield.   It was Eva's smile.

The car doors swung open noiselessly.   The neighborhood waited, but there was none of the usual scene.   Rather, the aristocrats disembarked, and head held high Eva came around the car to stand beside Charles.   Beaming with pride, she couldn't contain her excitement.   "Look at what Chuck bought us this morning.   Isn't he just the nicest boy?" she said, her fingers running over the worn but clean upholstery of the driver's seat.

Charles was obviously proud, too, but his wasn't the pride that comes with possessing a new car.   It really couldn't be because, though a vast improvement over the old, this one was still a ten-year-old castoff.   But Charles was proud that his son would bother to ask him and Eva downtown for lunch and would spend some time with them before taking them to a dealer to buy the car.   This had all come about on the third day after Chuck and his wife had visited Charles and Eva.   Once more, the old couple had a car, given as proof of the son's love.   Chuck never came back to visit them again.

Chapter 8

The windows were dark, the dust on them reflecting the trash in the gutter of Magazine Street. The shelves behind the flaking sign reading HARDWARE STORE were barren. The windows were always dark and the shelves were always barren, but the door was never closed. Today, it was.

"Nothing like rent due to bring out a landlord," Charles frequently griped. But when McLaughlin didn't show up as usual on the first day of the month, Charles was the first to suggest that he and Steve go check on him. "He's old, you know. Living in that ratty old store by himself, you never know."

Steve tentatively opened the door and peered down the rows of dust-laden shelves, past the piles of screws in half-rotten boxes, around a table covered with generation-old appliances, and into the gloom at the rear of the store. A red glow from a cigar moved slowly as McLaughlin looked up from his seat at the poker table where he ran nightly games. The only decent piece of furniture in the place, the normally cleared table was now covered with bursting files, a coffee-stained ledger book, wads of crumpled paper, and a bourbon bottle.   McLaughlin slumped in an old wooden desk chair that tilted precariously leftward, cotton hanging from a tear in the pillow that he used to bring his butt back on level.   The landlord looked drained and far older than his sixty-seven years.   His normally fat body had collapsed even further into his belly, and there had not been enough alcohol in the now-empty bottle to bring color to his face.   His vein-mapped hands lay helplessly on the table.

"Well, boys," he acknowledged their presence, hesitating and visibly swallowing.   "It's all over.   I can't go on with it.   I don't have the money to do what they're ordering."   The words, once started, rushed out of his bloated, old face.   "I don't want to.   God, how I don't want to, but I've got to sell your place." He nodded toward a letter open on top of the pile in front of him.

Office of the Inspector
City Hall
New Orleans, Louisiana

Harry McLaughlin
_____Magazine Street
New Orleans, Louisiana

Subject: Violation of City Housing Codes

Dear Sir:

In response to allegations by the Camp Street Improvement Association, the city inspector has examined your property located at _____ Camp Street and found numerous violations of city housing codes. You have ten (10) days from the date of this letter to correct the violations listed below. In accordance with NOLA 67-101, if the violations are not corrected in the ten day period, you are subject to criminal prosecution under Criminal Statute 92-5736.   The penalty is a maximum of six (6) months imprisonment and five thousand dollars ($5,000) fine per violation.

(1) NOLA 51-1559:   Unsafe entryways. Specific complaints include improper railing on stairways and deteriorating porch flooring.

(2) NOLA 52-336:   Improper lighting in multiple dwelling hallways.   Specific complaints include no entry hall light found or apparent wiring for provision of such light.

(3) NOLA 52-1398:   Unsanitary solid disposal: Specific complaints include leakage of sewerage into lower apartment from upper apartment.

Plumbing does not meet minimum standards of city code.

(4) NOLA 67-782:   Improper rear

access.   Specific complaint is that collapsed walkway on the side of house restricts egress and ingress in case of fire.

(5) NOLA 69-472:   Improper street frontage maintenance: Specific complaint is that walkways are not kept free of debris and, therefore, pose a hazard to pedestrians.

(6) . . . .

The list of code violations continued for three more pages.

"Well, when's he going to get here?" Al Isaacs asked as if his partner, Marc Isaacs, should know.   Al's spotless car stood out like a sore thumb from where they were parked in front of Charles' and Eva's apartment house, waiting for Harry McLaughlin to show up.   He was to have let them look at the place at nine o'clock.   It was now fifteen minutes past, and Al was irritated.

"Maybe he's backed out," Marc volunteered.

"Are you kidding?" Al was scornful.   "He's got no choice but to sell, and he deserves it, too.   I tried to be reasonable with him, made him a good offer, but, no, he wouldn't hear of it.   'Didn't want to sell at any price,' he said.   Can you believe that?   Wanted to know what he'd do with his time if he didn't have these apartments to look after.   Wanted to know what would happen to the tenants.   Yeah, like he really cares.   I'd have loved to have seen his face when he got that letter from the city.   They gave him ten days to repair all of the problems that they mentioned, or else he would face charges.   And that was some list that Lori came up with.   She did a hell of a job.   Those people spilled their guts to her about every little thing, and every one of them was in that letter."   Isaacs laughed.   "This is going to be a nice place," he continued, looking over at the house just in time to see a curtain close from where someone had been watching the two strangers.   "It's going to be so nice that I might even move here myself as soon as the rest of the neighborhood is cleaned up."

"What!   What do you mean 'you might move here'?" Marc snapped.   "You told Lori and me that you were going to move here.   That's the only reason she went to all the trouble of organizing the neighborhood association and making those inspections and interviews for you.   So, what're you saying, Al?"

"Later.   Later.   Here's McLaughlin, now."   Isaacs looked in the mirror as the landlord pulled up behind them in his rusted Plymouth.

McLaughlin waddled toward Al and Marc Isaacs as they moved to the sidewalk to wait for him.   His hands clutched a letter with the heading of the city government showing as he waved it at the two young men in front of him.

"Well, Isaacs, you little overdressed bastard, I guess you're going to get what you've been wanting, aren't you?"   The venom in the words belied McLaughlin's drained appearance.   "I know exactly what you're going to do here, and I hope you burn in hell for it. There are cockroaches running all over these old neighborhoods now that there's money in them, and you're all just alike.   Do anything for a buck, even get the government boys downtown on your side, won't you?"   McLaughlin spat out the words.

"Now, Harry, don't take it so hard."   Isaacs was in such a good mood that he was willing to overlook McLaughlin's slander.   "It's time you retired.   After all, how old are you now?   Seventy-five?   Seventy-six?   And besides, Harry, don't forget.   You could have done much better by this place yourself."   Isaacs didn't care if McLaughlin took offense at what he was saying.   He had laid the groundwork well, had the old man in a bind, and knew whatever he said wouldn't affect the sale.

McLaughlin ignored the comment and started up the steps to Charles' and Eva's apartment.   As he was raising his fist to knock on their door, Isaacs suddenly barged ahead of him and grabbed the doorknob to open it.   With surprising agility, McLaughlin roughly shoved the smaller man aside and blocked the door with his own body.   "What do you think you're doing, Isaacs?   I don't care who you are.   You don't barge in on these folks without knocking first.   Besides," McLaughlin paused to knock on the door, "you're not getting in until I show everyone in the building this letter from the city.   And you're not getting in until you ask them nicely if they mind your looking at their place."

"Alright, Harry, whatever you say."   Isaacs smirked, rolling his eyes at his cousin.

In spite of McLaughlin's warning, they didn't ask if they could come in.   "We want to look at your place," one did say, unceremoniously, as the two young men pushed Charles aside.   They shoved the door past its normal arc and jammed it into the linoleum, and Charles watched as a sour-faced little man dressed flawlessly in a blue suit, pranced into the room and began to poke around.   The second, in slacks and sport shirt, taller than the first by at least a head, remained behind to unstick the door.   Failing in that, he followed the leader further into the apartment.

"Who is it, Charles?   Who's at the door?" Eva yelled from the back room.

"Just McLaughlin and some men wanting to look around," he answered, not wanting to upset her, but not knowing any more than she did.

"We just want to look at your place."   The taller one did smile but didn't add any details to what his companion had said when they had first barged in. Meanwhile, the little one was examining everything he came to, looking at every crack in the wall, stomping on the floor, pulling bricks from the fireplace grate, threatening to bring the entire chimney down into the living room.   A cloud of dust marked his path through the room.

Charles would probably have called the police if McLaughlin had not been with the two men.   The landlord was standing on the front porch gripping the railing, his head down, trying hard not to see the rape of Charles' and Eva's privacy.   He made no effort to explain what was going on.   Perhaps he was unable to explain.   His presence, however, meant that whatever this visit was, it was with his permission.

They weren't inspectors, Charles could tell that. Inspectors rarely inspect, at least not like these two were doing.   Besides, inspectors don't come in expensive clothes like the little one was wearing.   He was flawlessly groomed, his dark suit complementing perfectly his swarthy complexion and his black hair styled so as to reduce its noticeable curl.   His companion, although dressed more casually, was also just as perfectly clothed.   His most distinctive characteristic was his smile that was constant regardless of what was said or done.   A pleasant looking fellow, one hand in his pocket and motioning with the other, he tagged along like a puppy behind his more stern companion.

They were worse than inspectors would have been. They yanked open closet doors and dragged the contents into the room so as to reach the walls of the closet.   Pans were emptied from shelves under the sink and left in the floor to be tripped over by the near-blind Eva.   The toilet was flushed constantly for several minutes.   Ignoring the food cooking on and in the stove, the little one repeatedly turned the burners off and on and the oven up and down.   The back screen door was jerked from one hinge by a particularly hard pull, and a picture was dropped while the wall behind it was being examined.   All of this was done without comment, apology, or even acknowledgment of the existence of Charles and Eva.

"I'm sorry for any inconvenience we may be causing you, but we'll only be a few more minutes," the smiling one finally said something to them.   He grinned broadly as he did, as if such invasions of privacy were just another ordinary day's events.   "You know," he continued, "you and Mrs. Pruitt have a very nice apartment here.   You're fortunate to have such a place."

Charles couldn't believe what he was hearing as his

eyes scanned the faded wall paper, the worn linoleum, and the huge chunks of missing plaster.   Added to that, now, were clothes and pots left in the floor by these two and a suitcase pulled from under the bed along with a huge pile of dust dragged with it.   It was too much to comprehend.   Weariness settled over him, a fatigue of the mind that made him too tired to even think of words for responding to such a ridiculous statement.   Rather than try, he went out on the porch to stand beside McLaughlin.

"What's going on, Mac?   Who are these guys?" Charles asked.

"You saw the letter the other day, Charles.   I've got to sell, and they're thinking about buying it.   The little guy's Al Isaacs, a real smuck if there ever was one, and the taller one's his cousin, Marc.   It's people like them who've already bought up the places between here and Audubon Park.   They're just maggots after meat, Charles, maggots after meat."   Mac's voice trailed off as the two Isaacs filed out the door.   Al Isaacs was brushing his jacket sleeves off and looking repeatedly at the palms and then the backs of his hands is if not believing the grime that had collected there.   His cousin, still smiling, began to brush off Al's back as the short man confronted McLaughlin.

"You've really got some nerve, McLaughlin, asking such a price for a place that brings in so little each month.   It's not worth risking my money for that small a return.   Personally, I can't figure out why, given the opportunity this place offers, you haven't made more from it.   Why haven't you charged more for rents?" Al Isaacs asked.

The old slum-lord's fingers showed white from

gripping the loose porch railing as he looked from the confused faces of Charles and, now, Eva to the rotten porch and chipped paint of the old house on to the overconfident, arrogant expression of this over-dressed, young lawyer.   He wanted to say "because it's a fair rent!   Because I wanted to make a living from it, not a killing!   Because these people need a place to live that is cheap, and they depend on me not to raise rents!   Because ..., because ..., because."   He had so many answers.   He had already asked himself the same question hundreds of times.

Repeatedly, he had started to raise the rents, but he just couldn't bring himself to do it.   He'd been raised in the Irish Channel, and he knew what it was like to be poor.   He'd been in Charles' and Eva's apartment and all the others at collecting time, and he knew they lived on the absolute margin.   Besides, it just wasn't right for him to make money off of people when he'd almost been handed the property.   If Interstate 10 had not taken the old home place and if the government hadn't paid more for the land than it was worth, he'd never have owned the house.   So, each time he considered raising the rent, he would back out.   He just couldn't do it.

Instead of the angry words that Isaacs' question deserved, he said nothing.   He had to sell the place, and this little ass and his smiling lackey were his only offer.   He gritted his teeth and held back.

The little man strode across the porch to the door of the next apartment while the smiling one hung behind to mop up after the dirty work.   "Thank you for your trouble and for letting us barge in like this," he said. "I apologize for any inconvenience."   With his part of the job finished, he turned and trailed after his leader, leaving McLaughlin behind.

With a plainly visible effort, the old landlord managed to raise his head but found it hard to look at Charles and Eva where they remained huddled together in the entry hallway listening to the conversation.   He couldn't meet their eyes.   He knew he was letting them down, and he wanted to die.   For a few seconds he tried desperately to think of something to say that would make right what he was doing.   He gave up, dropped his head, and hurried after the two young men who, without having knocked, were twisting on the door knob, trying to get into Mike's apartment.

"Don't drive away too fast," Marc ordered as the two of them got back to their car.   "I want to talk about that last comment you made before McLaughlin arrived, what you said about 'you might move here.'   What do you mean 'you might ....'?"

"Okay, we'll talk, but not here.   Right now, we need to get away from here.   Those people were awfully unhappy about McLaughlin selling the place, especially that big guy, Mike."

"We shouldn't have let McLaughlin show that letter to everyone and let them know Lori had tricked them. That one woman, that young one in the big guy's apartment.   I've never heard a woman curse like that before.   I believe she would have torn Lori's head off if she'd been with us."   Marc was still rattled.

"Well, it just goes to show the kind of people we're dealing with here.   Scum.   Pure scum," Al Isaacs interjected.

"Okay, but what about you?   Are you moving here

or not?"   Marc wouldn't be put off.   "Your head is the one that is going to be torn off if Lori thinks you've misled her," he continued, already knowing from Al's avoiding the question how he was going to answer.

"You'll help her get over it," Isaacs grunted. "Look, you agreed to go into this with me.   It's too good an opportunity to pass up, and this is just the beginning.   It's a beautiful situation, you know.   We pick up these old houses for a song, put a little money into them to meet codes, then turn around and sell them for a quick profit to somebody else who wants to put the real money into their restoration, maybe to live in themselves.   Everybody's doing it; I've got to get in on it."

"Yes, I know I agreed to handle a lot of the details for you.   But the understanding was that this first one was to be for you to move into as a home.   Buying and selling was to be discussed later.   Besides, how are you going to swing something like this financially?   If you're not going to move into it while you're fixing it up, like Lori and I did, then it's going to be sitting a while without any income.   I know you're doing well financially, but I am your accountant, you know, and unless you've gotten rich in the last couple of days, I'm guessing that you're borrowing the money to buy the house.   So, how are you going to swing the payments without any income on the place?"

"Oh, but I will have income while it's being remodeled."   Al laughed.   "You saw how scared those people back there were that they were going to get kicked out.   Well, I'm going to do them a favor. They're going to get a notice from me that will invite--I repeat--invite them to stay on.   I'll keep them on with a few promises while we work.   Once the remodeling is done, then, we'll get rid of them."

Marc shifted uncomfortably.   "That's kind of rough on them, isn't it?   You're planning to put them through the problems that go with remodeling, give them hope that they'll be able to stay on, and then kick them out?"

"Toughen up," Al scolded his cousin, slapping the car seat impatiently.   "Look.   We're doing the city a favor.   We're bringing money back into this end of town like no government program has ever done. We're revamping these neighborhoods and getting professionals to return as residents.   They're increasing the tax base and the occupational income base as well.   I mean, they ought to be giving us medals for doing this.   Besides," Al Isaacs continued, "this trash needs to be run out.   They're just a bunch of welfare chiselers.   And furthermore, my dear cousin," he added, sarcastically, "if it bothers you that I'm kicking out these people, you did exactly the same thing when you bought your place.   You might not have seen it directly, but how many apartments were in your house when you bought it?   Five?   Six?   How many people lived in that one building?   Ten? Twenty?   Twenty-five?   And, now, how many live there?   You, Lori, and Kim!   Three of you replaced all those other people.   So, you've put a few people on the street too, my friend."   Al paused to let his words sink in.   "Ah, don't look like that," he said, seeing that Marc was suddenly looking very uncomfortable.   He didn't want some crisis of conscience suddenly interfering with his plans.   "Don't worry about it.   They won't really go live on the street.   They'll get someplace else to stay.   And as for us?   Well, we'll have money in our pocket, and we can be proud of what we've helped the city to do."

Chapter 9

After leaving the insurance business, Charles took up woodworking as a way of making a living. Now, in his old age, it was only rarely that someone would hire him to do a little work. Still, an occasional job brought in a little extra cash to help out. Key to his ability to do this work were his tools and a small supply of fine lumber that he kept stored in a shed at the back of the tenement house.

Lately, the number of thefts in the area had made Charles begin to worry more about break-ins. So, on this particular morning he was on his way down the side of the apartment house to the storage shed to think about bringing what he had there into the house. He knew he would probably never actually move the stuff because he'd gone back there three times already to get it. Each time he had come back empty-handed. But, going there and mulling over whether to carry it or not got him out of the house and out of Eva's way for a while. Besides, the old shed had a great seat to rest on.

Like many of the houses in this part of the city, this one had been built before the widespread adoption of indoor plumbing.   Each house had been built with the "little shack out back" commonly associated with rural areas.   Each of the sheds had a toilet seat with a hole leading directly into the sewer below, and these seats made a fine place to sit and think, or sit and drink, or whatever.   It never ceased to amaze Charles at how new-looking the seat was after all the years of use. But, he thought, smiling at the image, it was probably never sat on for very long.   Everyone was afraid the sewer rats would bite them on the ass.

For a moment, he paused to listen to a rooster crowing loudly in the cool of the early morning.   The sound was not alien to the city as several tenement houses had their hidden chicken coops behind them. But he always stopped to listen in amazement as the crowing penetrated the sounds of the traffic of Magazine Street, spiraled above the walls of houses which attempted to restrain it, and swept down on unsuspecting pedestrians to give them pause.   So concentrated was Charles on this particularly raucous cock that he nearly stumbled over the legs sticking out from under the house and blocking his way.

His heart felt like it skipped a beat at the shock of seeing the unexpected.   It wasn't the first time someone had crawled under there and startled him. Usually, it was some wino who'd wandered down this way from Lawrence Square.   Once, some kids had stuffed a dummy under there.   Both the winos and the dummy wore castoff jeans and worn out tennis shoes. The legs getting Charles' attention were dressed in expensive slacks, matching socks, and well-shined loafers, and their owner was saying something unintelligible.

The mystery unraveled a second later as Charles spied Al Isaacs standing just around the back corner of the house.   But, of course, Charles thought, I should have recognized that fancy car of his setting out front. The little man was out of his suit, looking distinctly uncomfortable without it, and Charles noted with amusement the dress slacks and white shirt in which the lawyer had come to work.   His physical effort at the moment consisted of pushing a pen across a pad each time there came a burst of words from Marc Isaacs, the one, as it turned out, with the dirty job under the house.

"Ah, Mr. Pruitt," Al Isaacs said, surprising Charles with his friendly tone.   "It's good to see you this morning.   What we're doing is going over the place to see what we need to do to it.   In a few days, there'll be some workmen in here getting the critical needs met. Some of the lower priority problems will be scheduled for a month or two from now.   So, strangers you see around will be the workers that I've sent.   I would appreciate your passing on to the other renters that nothing has changed here except the owners, and that we are going to be working hard to make it a better place to live."   He turned away without waiting for Charles to reply.   "Oh," he turned back to him.   "I almost forgot to tell you.   I will be leaving a note in each of your mailboxes with the address where to send the rent."

Charles started to say something but saw that Isaacs was paying no attention.   He turned and shuffled back toward the front of the house.   He felt uneasy and had lost his appetite for looking in the shed. It was natural to be anxious when a change was being made that could leave Eva and him living on the street. But Isaacs had just been reassuring and reasonable, and Charles should have been feeling better.   He wasn't.   There had been something he couldn't pinpoint in the exchange that had left him with a sense of dark foreboding.   A chill ran up his spine as he tried to puzzle it out.   Then it came to him, not the answer as to what was wrong, but the answer as to why he felt something was wrong.   During the entire conversation that they had just had, Isaacs had been smiling.   It was an expression that Charles had never seen before on the landlord's face.   Now that he had, he didn't think he wanted to see it again because it lent the young man an especially sinister look.   It was a smile that was little more than a grimace of the lips, a necessary gesture for the moment, an act with no reflection in the eyes.

"Charles, we've got a letter!   We've got a letter! We've got a letter from Mr., uh, Mr., uh, Mr. Isaacs!" Eva was the only one who called him mister even though she could hardly remember his name.

Charles, Mike, and Steve were sitting on the porch when Eva burst out of the house waving an envelope in the air.   Charles was instantly alert; it had to be something awful for Eva to appear in public in her ragged beige slip, barefooted, with hairpin plastered head.   But her shout was light and joyful and her walk was a dance of happiness.   She could have been a kid off to school as she almost skipped across the porch to hand him the letter.   His eyes followed her in wonder back into the house, and he remained thus until the cool sensation of smooth, expensive stationery against his fingers shook him from his reverie.   Unconsciously shaking his head, he glanced at the sheet of paper.   It was on the letterhead of Isaacs' law firm.

Mr. and Mrs. Charles Pruitt
_____ Camp Street
New Orleans, Louisiana

Dear Mr. and Mrs. Pruitt:
This is to inform you that I have purchased the property located at _____ Camp Street from Harry McLaughlin.   At Mr. McLaughlin's request, all tenants in the building are being informed that they will be allowed to continue renting as you have done in the past.   I trust that you will decide to continue as a tenant under my ownership.

Let me apologize ahead of time for any inconvenience that you may be caused by the improvements that will be made on the property.   As you know, a number of repairs must be made in order to meet the requirements of appropriate city codes.   In addition, I will be improving the property in other ways which will make it a much better place to live.

If you have any questions about this, feel free to contact either Marc Isaacs or me.

Sincerely,

Alford Isaacs
Attorney-at-law

The verbal assurances from Isaacs had meant nothing to Charles; he didn't trust the little man as far as he could see him.   Having him state it on paper, though, meant something.   Here it was in concrete, signed, sealed, and delivered.   He and Eva would have a place to live.   Charles breathed a deep sigh, and, suddenly, he was struck by the joy that had lightened Eva's feet and propelled her onto the porch.   It was the relief of awakening from a horrible dream, the relief of surviving a battle in war, the relief of the new convert whose sins have been lifted from a burdened soul.   It was a sensation that flowed outward from his abdomen, engulfing him, pulling him erect, squaring shoulders long since permanently slumped, and making his legs and feet fidget with the desire to run, to jump, to dance without purpose or direction, for pure joy.   He let himself smile.   He couldn't help but smile as he turned to the others to explain.   There was no need.   Wordlessly, the message had already been conveyed, and Mike and Steve were scrambling for their mailboxes to get their own promises of security.

Normally, Eva's trips away from the house took hours of preparation.   In her excitement at the good news from Isaacs, though, she shed the slowness of years.   Before the hubbub of Steve and Mike's own letter opening had subsided, she was back out the door dressed in her best.

"Come on, Charles," she ordered, practically dragging him off the steps as she hardly slowed to grab his arm.   "We're going to keno."

The usual fuss that would follow such an interchange didn't occur.   Charles, still smiling broadly, recovered his balance and trailed Eva toward the car.   Still struck dumb by this sudden good fortune, he could only wave when the lawyer from across the street staggered to the sidewalk to shout a greeting.

Mike and Steve remained behind on the porch, and they were still there chatting, joking, and laughing when evening fell and the dwellings began to disgorge their occupants onto the porches and sidewalks and street.   The news of good fortune diffused through the block, and the clumps here and there gradually congregated around Mike and Steve.   Beer began to appear in six packs and cases from refrigerators, coolers, and the trunks of cars.   The cans began to pile up in the gutter, on the edge of the porch, and on the Crane's patch of grass.   Gallon jugs of Thunderbird wine were circulated, contributed by a distant neighbor five houses away, and the party was on.

It was a night to remember as people laughed and cried, hugged and kissed, argued, supported, and added creative memories to the many stories told of their lives together.   The sounds of people silently doing the Mardi Gras hop to the totally unnoticed inappropriateness of country music blaring from the lawyer's wife's radio were mixed with bursts of wild laughter at the continuous antics of pranksters and the oft-told jokes of punsters.   Kids wove their way through the forest of legs, stealing the last swallows of beer from dropped cans, and the neighborhood cats and dogs risked their lives in the sea of trampling feet in order to capture some of the affection flowing from the crowd.   It was a members-only event, staged by and for those who had existed in this place for so long. Cars would slow for the crowd, then speed away, disconcerted and afraid of the mob that they thought had nearly caught them.   The only outsider was the TV newswoman and her dog.   She was so drunk when she bumped into the crowd that it took a while to convince her that she was not at a political convention and was not supposed to be reporting on the events.   Her own personal bottle of Thunderbird and a seat on the steps with Mike quickly brought her around, and she discovered that, although long forgotten, she had been at many of the events described.   With her reporter's skill, she was soon adding to many of the stories about the neighborhood.   No one could remember her having been where she said, but her added details were amusing and her slurred chatter was a welcome addition to the din of the party.

A damp fog from the river hung between the street lamp and the winking eyes of a thousand beer cans and bottles when, later that night, Charles and Eva coasted into the curb.   Glass crunched under the tires as they stopped, and three cats, startled from their feast, strewed crawfish hulls across the walk as they streaked away.   The upright Augustine grass of the Crane's yard had finally given up under the stomping of excited feet and sat bowed and crumpled.   Food scraps spotted the curb and combined with the stench of stale beer and already rotting seafood.

Charles and Eva sat in stunned silence, transfixed by the devastation.   But there was no tirade from Eva. There was no hard set of the jaw from Charles as he picked his way through the ruins toward his door, for the full story was here.   From out of the fog wending its way through the darkness of the alleys came the whisper of laughter and a scent of the joy that had been here tonight.   Charles and Eva smiled at the knowledge.   They also smiled because, at keno, Eva had won her biggest pot.

Chapter 10

The tenement house on Camp Street became a beehive of activity as the two Isaacs wasted no time in turning work crews loose on the place. As the pace picked up, Charles and Eva found themselves continually dodging piles of boards left here and there. Dust kicked up by the constant shaking of the house by one task or another attacked their eyes and noses, and Eva lived with a handkerchief constantly pressed over her face. Parking space was limited as the trucks became increasingly dominant, and the walk to their car became longer and more troublesome as they had to park further down the block. In spite of the trouble, they believed it would be short-lived, and spirits that had risen with Isaacs' letter remained high.

Charles' normal morning ritual was to go out onto the front porch to stand for a few minutes, work out the nighttime kinks, and say a hello to anyone who was about. On this particular morning, he found his nearest neighbor, Steve, staring at broken pieces of a lock and chain scattered about the porch floor.   "They got my bike," Steve said, explaining the glum look on his face.

Charles didn't bother suggesting Steve call the police.   Both men knew they would probably never come.   The bike was just gone for good and there was nothing to be done about it.   It was surprising, actually, that the theft had not occurred before.   The bike had been kept on an open front porch in an area of New Orleans where anything not tied down was likely to disappear, and it had been there for two years. Once in that time, a front wheel had been taken from it, but, miraculously, nothing more.

The neighborhood was accustomed to theft.   Once, Steve had worked all day putting a tape player in his car only to have it stolen that very night.   Charles' tools were taken from his trunk and the Slovak's car was stolen from in front of her house.   The alcoholic lawyer's went the same way, which was quite a joke considering it would barely run.   It wasn't so funny, however, when it was figured out that the thieves had gotten the keys to the car by jimmying open a window on the lawyer's apartment and taking them from the wife's purse while she was asleep.

Theft could be handled, though it caused inconvenience.   Even the teenagers who sold stolen goods door-to-door had become a more-or-less accepted part of the scene and occasionally made sales on the block.   But the threat of personal violence that had become part of the thefts couldn't be accepted. This added dimension was frightening, and the stories surrounding assaults and attacks became a major part of neighborhood lore.   One of the women renting above the alcoholic lawyer had been raped in her apartment by someone who was burglarizing the place. The Cranes had been terrorized by a robber who had threatened to kill them, and Mr. McConnell, the bachelor who lived on the other side of the Cranes, had been carried out in a body bag after having been shot and left to die a slow death that the cops estimated took two days.

There was a feeling of helplessness in the face of the violence. Calling the police did no good for it took them an hour or two to arrive, and they never seemed to catch anyone. So people in the neighborhood just put up with the theft and tried to stay alive. More and more, they would do what the couple living above Charles and Eva had done when they came home one afternoon to find their apartment door open and a burglary in progress. They simply walked down the street to wait until it was over and they could safely return home to count their losses. So a theft of a bicycle was nothing. Charles and Steve were just glad they had not happened along while it was being taken.

Mike came out of his place just in time to hear Steve throw out a few appropriate curse words about the people who had ripped him off. "No, wait a minute!" he exclaimed. "Your bike wasn't stolen. I saw .... I saw .... I can't remember his name, but it's the fellow who just finished some of the work here for Isaacs. I saw him load the bike on his truck right at dark last night as he was leaving. I didn't say anything to him because I just thought you had sold it to him or something. I didn't think .... You mean you didn't?" Mike stammered. "Why, that son-uv-a-bitch ...," he cursed as the truth hit him. Mike was embarrassed at having let the rogue escape from under his nose.

"There's some mistake.   There's got to be." Isaacs was solicitous when Steve called him a few minutes later.   "Carlisle is a fine fellow who has worked for me several times.   I just can't believe ....   In fact, I know that he wouldn't take anything like that.   You say Mike thinks he saw him?"

"No," Steve said.   "Mike doesn't think he saw him. Mike knows he saw him."

"Well now," ice crept in to Isaacs' voice.   "There's a mistake here, and I know Carlisle ...."   He let his voice trail off meaningfully.   "But, I tell you what I'll do." Warmth flowed back into his words.   "I'll call him tonight, ask him about it, and get back with you in the morning.   How's that?"   The conversation ended.

Of course, Carlisle didn't take the bike, and Mike had been mistaken.   Of course, Carlisle was hurt that Isaacs would even question his integrity and didn't want to work for Isaacs anymore if he was going to be a suspect.   Of course, he was angry that tenants would accuse him, and he had a mind to go over there right now and punch Mike's big mouth.   But, of course, Isaacs talked him out of it and assured him that he had never doubted Carlisle but was only calling to cool down the tenants.

Isaacs' secretary rang up Steve the next morning and transferred the call to her boss.   "Steve," Isaacs began, "Carlisle said he was really sorry about your bike being taken, but he didn't know anything about it.   His only suggestion was that you might check with some of the contractors who are doing renovations further down the street.   Maybe it was one of them Mike saw. Their trucks look a lot alike.   I'm sorry that he couldn't turn up anything for us, but I really didn't think it would be otherwise."

Steve hung up slowly.   He, also, had not thought that it would be otherwise.

Charles and Eva had been out to the grocery for a few hours, and, having gotten some unexpected bargains, they were returning home in especially good moods. A smell of something burning tickled their noses while they were still on the sidewalk, but it was difficult to tell where it was coming from, and there was no smoke in evidence.   Neither of them thought too much about it until they opened their apartment door.   They could only stare at the destruction.

Without giving any notice to the occupants, Isaacs' workmen had let themselves in, yanked Charles' and Eva's sparse furnishings into the middle of the floor, and begun to strip the plaster walls of the many layers of paper and paint that covered them.   With special blowtorches, they had burned off the walls, their success in the process reflected in the piles of soot and ashes that covered everything.   Strips of partially burned paper were coiled everywhere and ashes swirled around his ankles as Charles stooped to pick up one. The faded wallpaper had looked bad, but it had been wonderful compared to the partially charred plaster that now decorated the apartment.   The stench was nearly unbearable.

"How long before your workers will be back to clean up here?" Charles questioned Al Isaacs over the phone a few minutes later.   He had located him at his cousin's house and, after explaining the situation to Marc, been turned over to Al.

"Well, now.   They won't be back to clean up."
Isaacs snorted.   "I'm certain that they didn't mess
things up that badly.   I've used these men before, and
they've always done a good job.   They will be back on
Monday morning, though, to finish the job, and I'm
sure they would appreciate it if you would have any
furniture moved out of the way so they can work."

Charles had hesitated to call Isaacs and bother him.
"After all," he'd said, "he is just trying to help us."   But
any hesitation on his part was rapidly giving way to
anger and disbelief the longer the little man talked.
"Now, Isaacs," he said, "this smell is awful in here.
Eva and I can hardly breathe for it.   You mean to tell
me there's nothing your men can do to clear this up?"

"Just open your windows," Isaacs answered.
"You'll just have to put up with it for now."   The line
went dead as he hung up on Charles.

"Damn!"   Al slammed his coffee cup down on Marc's
kitchen table as he hung up the phone and turned back
to his cousin.   "I'm getting tired of their complaining
all the time.   First they gripe about a few minor
possessions that they claim the carpenters ripped off
when all their possessions together aren't worth a fig.
Then, they complain about the inconvenience.   It's so
dusty they can't breathe, they claim.   If I didn't need to
keep them in there a while longer, I swear I'd kick the
bunch of them out right now."

"You may not have to kick them out," Marc said.
"They may just leave.   Charles sounded pretty upset to
me.   Before I handed you the phone, he said there was
soot all over everything and a terrible stink.   He said,
too, that somebody has gone through their dresser

drawers and some things are missing.   It doesn't sound like a place I would want to live."

"Well, he can get upset all he wants," Al said. "Those two aren't going anywhere.   Some of the tenants might be able to afford to leave, but the Pruitts will be with us until the end, the very end.   You watch."   Al grinned.

"What do you think they're going to say when your men tear the porch off the house and take down the shed that's in the back?   The tenants have been using those for storage."   Marc had a hard time believing that there were people who would put up with such harassment indefinitely.

"Well, to get the highest dollar for this place, I've got to put it back like it was when originally built. That porch was added on later, and the shed was enlarged from its original size.   So, they've both got to be torn down, whether the tenants like it or not."   Al explained.   "By then it really doesn't matter what they think.   We'll be within a couple of weeks of finishing the project, and that's when I'm going to raise their rent.   As much as it's going up, they won't be staying anyway.   I tell you what, Marc," Al continued.   "Let's shut them up now, so we don't have to put up with anymore of their complaining.   Call them and tell them that if they don't like what is going on there, then they can leave anytime.   That'll be the end of it.   I bet we won't hear from them again.   Oh," Isaacs noticed his cousin's lack of enthusiasm for the suggestion, "if you don't want to do it, then I'll take care of it myself. I'll take care of them, but I'll wait until they call again. When they do, they're going to get a real surprise."

Chapter 11

The sun was warm, and the humidity for this time of year was very bearable. It was a great time for a walk, and Steve meandered through the New Hope's territory, peeking through fence slats into their ivy-covered, walled gardens and letting his eyes walk down their bricked side paths. He enjoyed ambling along, admiring the polished brass of the mail slots and the ornate ironwork of the fences along the way, wondering as he went what it would be like to live in such a place. He ambled, but rarely stopped, because he knew if he moved too slowly it would only be a few minutes until the police showed up. He was out of his place and knew it

Returning home, he wasn't paying a lot of attention when he passed the Slovak's house, but he immediately sensed something was wrong. Men up on long ladders were leaning against the front of his house, but that was normal now with all the renovation going on. But the ladders were too far away from the street, he noticed.   Usually, they were set up with the base at the curb and the ladder leaning over the sidewalk and against the porch.   Now, the bases of the ladders were on the house side of the sidewalk, and that was impossible.   They couldn't lean against the building like that because the enclosed porch on the second floor of the building protruded out nearly to the sidewalk.   The porch was in the way.   But the porch .... Where's the porch?   Then he saw what remained of it piled on the back of one of the trucks that daily seemed to be hauling away pieces of their lives.   He'd had tools on the second floor of the two-story porch, some boxes of books, lawn chairs.   His cats were kept there.   It was all gone, in only a couple of hours. Along with Charles and Eva, who had just pulled up, he stood and watched as the porch was hauled away.

"Isaacs is out," his secretary said, responding to Steve's angry demand to talk to him.   His message for Isaacs to return his call went unanswered.   After trying a couple of more times, Charles tried his hand at it.   He reached Isaacs' office just in time for the secretary to convey the message that her boss had instructed her to pass on if a tenant called again.   "I don't have time to listen to anymore baseless complaints when I am trying to make your building a better place," she read.   "It seems to me that people like you should be appreciative of the efforts I am making on your behalf.   If you cannot be so, then I suggest that you find another place to live."

The message was stunning.   From the jubilation of being told they could stay, now came this.   Isaacs had just told them to either shut up or get out.   Charles slowly hung up the phone.   A sense of helplessness crowded in on him, and he felt his anus constrict and just as suddenly loosen, threatening to release the contents of his bowels into his pants.   The feeling scared him.   He'd had it often when he was a kid, when he'd been so afraid of his dad's beatings that a mere threatening gesture from him was enough to make Charles mess his pants.   At age fourteen, he had walked away from his family vowing that no human would ever make him lose control like that again.   No one had, until now.   At age seventy-nine, almost eighty, he was helpless once again.   What did Isaacs want, and what would he do next?

A few days after the porch was ripped off, Charles got up to find a large truck squeezed into the alley between his house and the Cranes next door.   "Morning, podnah," the older member of the work crew hollered at Charles as he rounded the house to see what was going on.   "The boss sent us over here to clean up this mess," he announced cheerfully, emphasizing his words with the clatter of lumber he had just tossed into the back of the truck.   "Yessir, we're going to clean it up, going to clean this mess right up, gonna make this uh place as uh good as uh new."   He lapsed into a rhythmic singsong as he swung board after board. And he and his crew did as he'd said.   By early afternoon, the truck was gone leaving the place looking vastly neater after the days of clutter.

"Mr. Pruitt, have you seen Mike's lawn mower?" Steve asked.   He was standing in the open door of Charles' and Eva's apartment, a worried look on his face.   "I was going to borrow it, but it's gone out of the shed."

Charles feet hit the floor with a thud as he swung off the bed where he had been laying.   Something hadn't been right.   He'd known it as soon as he had talked to the workmen.   They had been too friendly, or they had refused to meet his eyes, or something.   But he had sensed that something was not right.   The shed.   Mike's lawnmower.   What else had they cleaned out on Isaacs' orders?

Moments later, his eyes confirmed the sinking feeling he'd already had.   Everything was gone.   An old disconnected toilet stood alone on the concrete floor, a solitary item missing the company of the boards and tools and equipment that had surrounded it for years.   Mike's mower was gone.   It hadn't been much.   He'd paid five dollars for the old push machine at the St. Vincent's de Paul Thrift Store on Magazine Street.   But it had been good enough that, with much huffing and puffing and cursing, one had been able to push it around the house and mutilate the little bit of grass that managed to survive there.   Without the mower, the grass would have been knee-deep because McLaughlin sure wouldn't have taken care of it.   "This place is completely unfurnished," McLaughlin had said when renting it, and he had meant it.

Charles' loss was not so easy to take.   The few tools that remained after most had been stolen from his car had been here.   There had been pipes and clamps, guides and jigs, vises and glues of a master woodworker.   A small stack of fine lumber, carefully hoarded and meted out, had been to use on the infrequent occasions when someone would hire an old man.   He had not made much money in recent years with his skills, but the rare job he did get made him feel useful and brought back to him a sense of satisfaction from the past.   When he worked, he could come home tired in the evening as did others in the neighborhood and sit with them on the steps.   He would kick his stiff leg out more spryly than normal, and getting around didn't give him nearly as much trouble.   But now his tools, his supplies, everything was gone.   The shed had been stripped.   Overcome, Charles sank onto the toilet, his face in his hands.

With no words to say that might ease Charles' agony, Steve watched in helpless silence as a memory of how he had first met this man played before his eyes. There was the image of Mike telling the recently arrived Steve that his nearest neighbor was a woodworker named Charles.   There was the scene as Steve tentatively approached the neighbor to ask if he would mind taking the time to look at something he was working on that was causing him some problems. There was the portrait, frozen forever in Steve's mind, of the delighted smile on Charles' face as the old man tried not to appear too eager as he quickly answered in the affirmative.   Just by being asked to help he had been made to feel useful.

Moments after Charles' agreed, Steve returned with a contraption that had the older man scratching his head because he had never seen anything like it. About three feet long, the object had a shape strangely reminiscent of a woman's figure.   A piece of a guitar fret board integrated into the structure gave away that this was some kind of musical instrument, but it was strange to Charles.   He examined the poorly cut sound holes and joints where glue had squeezed out but said nothing.   He hardly knew the new tenant and didn't want to hurt his feelings.

"It's a dulcimer," Steve partially relieved Charles from his predicament.   At least, now, he had a label for what this thing was supposed to be.

"Sure, it's a dulcimer.   A real beauty at that," Charles responded, knowing that he'd never seen one of these in his entire life.

"It's a traditional Appalachian musical instrument," Steve explained, guessing correctly that Charles didn't know what it was.   "I grew up in the mountains of East Tennessee," he continued, "but never in my life had I seen one of these.   I'd never even heard of them, but on TV the other night they had a woman named Ritchie playing one and talking like everybody from Tennessee and Kentucky grew up with them.   I figured since I was from there I ought to have one too."   Steve laughed.   "Reckoned I'd missed out on something someplace.   So I got some books out of the library that had pictures in them of dulcimers and set in to make this one.   Here's the problem, though, that I wanted to ask you about.   I cut this piece wrong right here. What can I do about it?"

"Nothing," Charles answered after running his hands over the site of the mistake and looking at it carefully.   "Leave it alone, because you can't even see it.   Everybody makes that kind of mistake.   Why, when I was building boats, I messed up like that all the time.   But," Charles hesitated, "since we just met, I guess you don't know about any of that, do you?   The story is that after I got out of the insurance business, I took to building boats.   My partner and I built about every kind of wooden one that you can imagine.   We were doing real well, too, until he tried to use an electric saw outside one day when it was raining, and it killed him." Charles shook his head. "We were pretty good at it, but, you know, we never built a one that didn't have a mistake in it someplace. Usually nobody ever noticed but us."

"As a matter-of-fact," Charles grinned at the memory, "I guess you and me are a lot alike. I remember when I first started, we built a Lafitte skiff without hardly ever being near one, just had some pictures to go by. I had just retired from the insurance business, needed money bad, and a friend of mine said he knew a fellow who needed a skiff for shrimping. Well, we did it. Boy, did we ever build him a boat. You know the platform that extends off the back of a Lafitte skiff? The one where they work the nets from? Well, we didn't support it good enough, just kind of stuck it out there in space. The first time the poor fellow lifted a load from there, the platform broke off, and he ended up in the water. Damned near drowned, too. Word gets around in that business, and it must have been five years before we got another order to build a skiff." Charles laughed at the memory. "We got lots better, though. Yeah, we got lots better, and you will too. You just keep working on this dulcimer and don't worry about a little mistake here and there. It'll be pretty, and no one will ever notice."

"Can I show it to you again?" Steve asked. "I don't want to bother you, but I don't know anything about finishing wood, and I could use your help."

"Bring it down anytime." Charles tried hard not to appear too eager. "I'm not very busy. I'd like to take a look at it."

With that conversation, Charles' and Steve's relationship began.   Over time, they grew closer and closer, Charles confiding more and more in the younger man.   Eventually, he told Steve his deepest secret, one that others in the neighborhood never learned until the very end.

"Uh, Steve, there's something I want to tell you before you go."   The two of them had been talking on the porch when Steve had turned to go to his own apartment.   The words rushed from Charles like a kid confessing to his parents, and Steve suddenly felt as if their ages were reversed.   "Steve, Eva and me ... uh, we're not really married.   We just live together because that's the only way we can make ends meet with us living on Social Security.   The government will cut our checks if we get married, and we barely make it now as it is."   He stopped as suddenly as he had started, embarrassed by his confession.   "The neighbors don't know it," he continued after a moment. "They think we're married, but we're not, and I wanted you to know."   His voice trailed off.

Charles could have told Steve practically anything, and he would have been more prepared for it.   As it was, his head spun trying to work this new bit of information into his overall image of Charles and Eva. My gawd! he thought.   They're shacking up!   This little old man and woman that look like they could be anybody's grandma and grandpa are shacking up! People my age are supposed to live together, not people like Charles and Eva.   Steve's mind raced on until, suddenly, laughter welled up in him.   The incongruity of it all squeezed unbidden tears from his eyes as he fought to hold them back.   It was clear that this was an important moment for Charles, a momentous disclosure. Steve couldn't mess it up for him by laughing. Choosing his words carefully, he asked, "Why are you telling me this, Mr. Pruitt?" The age difference between the two was too great for first names; Steve had never called his neighbor Charles. "It doesn't make any difference to me if you and Mrs. Pruitt are married or not."

"Well, Steve," Charles spoke haltingly now, almost embarrassed at his words. "I like you a lot. We talk a lot, and you help me out, keeping my old car going, and stuff. So, what you think about me is important. And you see .... Well ...," he hesitated, "I don't want you to think that if I was going to get married, I would marry anybody as cantankerous as that old woman." Steve laughed in spite of himself.

Now, the younger man stood in the shed door watching as Charles buried his head in his hands, his tools and supplies gone, the last vestiges of hope draining from him. Steve should have said something to him, even gibberish, to fill the void, but he was speechless and unable to take his eyes from the spectacle of a human brought low. As he watched, suddenly a weight seemed to press in on him, compressing his lungs until his breath was so rapid and shallow as to appear nonexistent. Despair, utter and complete despair, filled him with its darkness. Hopelessness, a sense of torment without ending, overwhelmed him. But these feelings were nothing compared to the waves of fear, the awful well of panic that swept over him. It was a fear that the despair would continue, a total panic that he would experience the hopelessness he was feeling for a moment more.

Unable to stand it another second, he bolted into the sunshine, staggering with emotion, and watched as Eva, appearing from nowhere, shoved past him to get to Charles.   He followed them with his eyes as she helped the old man toward the house.

Steve never told Charles what had happened that day, never told him that for a brief instant, he had felt what it was like to be seventy-nine years old and trying to survive in the world of others.   Perhaps, Charles knew.   After all, the two of them were very close.

Chapter 12

Everyone in the neighborhood could recognize Mike a block away. Maybe it was the way light reflected off his bald head or his slightly hunch-backed, arms-drooping stance. More than likely it was simply the fact that he was huge. Wide and stout, always dressed in khakis with his sleeves rolled up over bulging muscles, there was no doubt about his occupation. He had to be a longshoreman. He was.

Lured out of the bayou country by the promise of regular jobs, old-man-Gaudet had first moved his clan along with his new son-in-law, Mike, into the house across the street where the preacher now lived. "We had the whole house, and it was much nicer then than now," Mike told the story. "After two of my kids were born, we moved up the street and stayed in that dump for twenty years," he pointed down the block. "Then, we moved here. You could say, yes, we've been here a long time."

After old-man-Gaudet's death, Mike became the

patriarch of the largest and most intact family in the neighborhood.   It was a close-knit one whose members supported each other when times were hard and shared the wealth when things were better. Fights were common, and the more noisy ones often spilled over onto the front porch of the tenement house to provide entertainment for the neighbors.   But a more common sight was Mike sitting in the porch swing with his arm around his unmarried daughter and her baby or walking with his thirty year old son to the bus stop to see him off to work.

Two men walking together down a city street would not normally attract attention, but the appearance of Mike and his son was so unusual that even after years of seeing them together and marveling that they could get along, neighbors still stopped to watch and smile at the spectacle.   The brawny Mike would have his arm around the shoulders of a little fellow who was so scrawny he was almost lost in his father's bulk.   Mike Jr. was a little, bird-boned, pale-skinned man who always insisted, summer and winter, on wearing bright blue, velvet-looking suits.   His hair was prematurely thinning, going the way of his dad's, and what there was he brushed straight up so that it waved softly on his head.   He lisped when he talked, and he walked with short, mincing steps, his ass tucked under from constantly warding off the pinching, groping fingers of the patrons in the gay bar where he worked.   His sexual preference was rarely mentioned and had been a part of local gossip only once when, at one of Mike's parties, the son's boyfriend had made a pass at a male neighbor.   Mike Jr. and the incensed wife of the neighbor had backed the offender into a corner where he had to be rescued and evicted by Mike.   The event was the highpoint of the party.

There were many hard years for the family with everyone having to work at anything they could find to pool together the money for rent and food and clothes, but they had hung on until things had gotten better. As for Mike, he had benefitted from his years of hard work on the New Orleans docks and from a strong union that had been the first to win a guaranteed wage for its members.   When there were no ships to load or unload, a fellow dockworker would come by, pick up Mike's union card, and take it to the union hall to have it stamped.   In this way, the pay checks kept rolling in, work or no work.

To Mike's credit the incessant human drive to move to suburbia had somehow passed him by, and, in spite of his financial security, he stayed in this poor neighborhood.   If he had left, he would have been like a fish out of water.   In a way, he was a man lost anyway.   After years of barely getting by, of doing without, of having to get family or neighborhood support for what he needed, he no longer depended on these connections for economic survival.   So, in a fever to rid himself of the money that threatened to separate him from the ties of a past that he had enjoyed, he spent it.   He gave it away, threw it away, and   burnt   it   with   a   lavishness   middle-class suburbanites could never afford or understand.

Even in poverty, Mike had been generous with what he had or could come by.   Tool sets, televisions, and car stereos--all marked with foreign names such as Toyota, Sony, and Panasonic--somehow made their way from the ships he had been unloading at the docks over to Camp Street to be handed out to neighbors. Now that he had dollars, these also were passed around along with the gifts of dock contraband.

Contradictory to the thrust of American consumerism, Mike didn't throw his money after possessions.   "Why buy a new car?" he answered, when asked why he didn't.   "My old one runs fine. Besides," and laughter overflowed his rough voice, "working on it gives several of the fellows around here something to do with their time."   Instead, Mike spent his good fortune on family, friends, and neighbors.

Charles and Eva were quickly introduced to Mike's largess upon moving into the tenement house.   One afternoon, shortly after arriving, Charles and Eva were both napping--"resting her eyes," Eva called it--when a delicious aroma crept into the room and tickled their noses into wakefulness.   The smell, more akin to the outdoor aroma of bacon sizzling slowly over an open campfire or freshly baked bread emerging from a country kitchen, seemed foreign to this inner city area. It erased for a while the pungent odor of burned food, stale sweat, and the acid tinge of rotting garbage that normally characterized the neighborhood and drew the couple wordlessly toward the open window through which the bait was wafting.   Minutes later, drawn by a hollered invitation from next door, they were sitting on their back steps watching Mike work feverishly over a huge skillet.   It was piled high with long, white, strips of potato that were rapidly taking on the golden, crispy hue of delicious french fries.   On the second run of this outdoor cooker that Mike had rigged to run off a hose from his gas water heater, he had a pile of steaks ready to serve with the fries.   Charles and Eva ate that night as they had not eaten in years; neither of them could remember the last time they had tasted steak

In addition to his neighborhood fry-outs and crab boils, Mike was well known for buying the local neighborhood bar out of Dixie beer and crawfish.   As usual, he never went to the bar alone.   His outings were family as well as neighborhood affairs.   Mike's wife, as a matter-of-fact, had been known to drink her husband under the table on occasion, and she and the kids and grandkids of all ages insured that the bar would do a good business on "Mike nights."

But of all the stories of Mike, his most legendary were his "runs-to-Memphis," and, as his financial status improved and the trips became more frequent, the number of neighbors who could brag about having been along on one of them increased.   It was easy to find out who had gone; it was more difficult to find out what had gone on.   Participants had a hard time remembering, only knowing that, yes, they'd been along and they were sure, whatever they'd done, it had been fun.   You couldn't have sent a spy to find out about the trips, either, because those who went along weren't selected ahead of time.   Mike's runs-to-Memphis were spontaneous events.   Whoever was standing around at the moment and could pack into the car after all essentials were loaded was invited.

The essentials consisted of a three inch foam pad with which Mike covered the bottom of the large trunk in his Ford.   In the center of this insulation pad went a fifty pound block of ice from a local ice house and around the block were scattered cases of Dixie beer packed in crushed ice.   These provisions, which were reached from the front via a large hole cut behind the back seat, constituted the essentials for the trips.

This disappearance of males from the neighborhood happened so frequently that someone could have been kidnapped and no alarm would have gone out from the wives or kids until the weekend was over.   The trips were accepted, and no harm was committed as the men who went couldn't remember what they had done anyway.   More importantly, they couldn't remember what anyone else had done either, so it was impossible for them to gossip and embarrass anyone.   True, the favored few were usually sick for a few days afterward, but this was overshadowed by their pride once they were up and around again.   After all, they'd been on a run-to-Memphis.

The paternal feeling that Mike felt for his family carried over to the neighbors, and he made it his business to know what was going on around the area. Evenings would find him moving around on the steps and sidewalks and up the alleys between the houses, from cluster to individual to family, talking and listening.   Anyone paying attention could follow his trail by the ripple of laughter that marked it.   He would ask about this one or that one.   If a neighbor wanted to gripe, Mike would gripe too.   If a joke was told, there would be a counter.   If there was illness, sympathy would be given, and an obviously depressed friend would find the support necessary to face another day.   Direct questions were rarely asked, but by the time Mike wandered off to the next porch, he would know what was bothering those he had just left.

As March went by, more and more of the evening conversations turned to Isaacs and his doings.

Everyone had their favorite spot of curb for parking, and the new owner had violated each at least once. The Cranes' manicured spot of grass had been littered with boards, and the Slovak just didn't like his looks. "He reminds me of a dirty Czech!" she said.   The drunken lawyer was aggravated because Isaacs had not responded warmly to his overtures as a fellow attorney. Thus, up and down the block the tension built.

Of all the tenants, Charles and Eva were the ones Mike looked after the most.   He saw them as the weakest and most vulnerable.   His conversations with them were longer and more pointed, and he experienced Al Isaacs' harassment a dozen times over through the eyes and trembling voices of the old couple.   The anger he expressed to others after having talked to Charles and Eva showed clearly that he was becoming increasingly concerned with the effects of Isaacs' actions on them.   As time progressed, Mike's face grew darker.

"You little fucker, I'm going to break your gawd-damned neck!"   The building throbbed like a drum as Mike pounded Isaacs repeatedly against the house.   "You son-uv-a-bitch!"   Bam!   "You've got no right!"   Bam!   "You think you're so muthafuckin' good!"   Bam!

Without knocking, Al Isaacs had just opened the door to walk into Charles and Eva's apartment when, next, his back and head were drumming against the wall and his feet were flailing helplessly like those of a ventriloquist's dummy.   His approach unnoticed, an enraged Mike had yanked Isaacs backward out the door, spun him in mid-air, and planted him against the side of the house as if he were stacking boxes on the docks.   He was screaming and jamming him in cadence: "You've got no gawddamned right to treat people like this!"   Bam!

Trailing along behind his cousin, Marc Isaacs' perpetual smile was suddenly snatched from his face. He began backing slowly toward his car, fearing that he was going to be next.   His eyes were roving wildly from side to side, looking for help, looking for an answer to this outburst.   All he saw was a street suddenly deserted, doors quietly closing, windows with veiled eyes.   No one intervened because Mike was only the spokesman.   His frustration was the feeling of the neighborhood.   His violence was only what the neighbors collectively desired.   In fact, he probably treated Al Isaacs better than the neighbors would have, for, suddenly, in a gesture that reflected the feeling of futility that swept over him, he relaxed, and the little man tumbled to the ground.   Mike turned his back as if to shed himself of the scum that he had left disheveled behind him.   His turning away also hid the tears of helplessness that ran down his cheeks and dripped onto his khaki shirt.

Chapter 13

The tenants knew there would be retaliation after Mike's frustration erupted in violence, and they prepared themselves for the arrival of the uniforms and blue flashing lights.   A day later, on the 21st of March, it was the crepe soles, short pants, and leather bag of the postman that brought Isaacs' revenge.   The letter was unexpected; Isaacs had caught them by surprise, and hands trembled as they opened the long, crisp, law office envelope that bore the landlord's return address. Perhaps the cops would have been better.   They could not have been more devastating than the message conveyed in the letter.

Stunned by what was read, each turned into himself momentarily, hiding behind closed doors.   It was only later in the day that they finally met up in the backyard to discuss their plight.   By then, their initial rage was dying, and they were subdued, helpless in the face of larger forces.   Only Steve, the youngest, believed that anything could be done about the situation, but his bravado was severely challenged in the presence of his more experienced elders.

"We can't pay it," Eva shrieked.   "It's robbery, and we don't have it.   The place isn't worth it anyway. What's he trying to do?"

"Yeah, well," Mike growled, "we might be able to come up with it, but even if we can, I'm not going to give it to that son-uv-a-bitch.   I'll move first.   It's ridiculous for him to double the rent starting April first. That's just a few days."

"He can't do that," Steve repeated for at least the tenth time.   "I tell you, he just can't do it.   It's against the law.   He has got to give us thirty days notice before he does anything like this.   I just know it."

"Come on, Steve," Mike remonstrated.   "The guy's a shyster.   He knows what he can and can't do with the law.   Besides, what're we going to do about it?   Sue him?   You got that kind of money?   I don't.   What we ought to do is burn the goddamned place to the ground."

Silence fell over them as each contemplated Mike's rage and each, in turn, repressed the urge to fuel the fire smoldering just below the surface in all of them. Charles had the letter on his knee, already stained and limp from the constant folding and unfolding of it during this long day.   He defused the loaded silence by beginning to quietly read the important part.

"Effective with the next rental payment that is due on April 1, your rent will be doubled.   In addition, there will be due a damage deposit equal to one month's rent that will be refunded to you in full upon your leaving if my inspection determines that the apartment has sustained no damage beyond normal wear and tear.   With your next month's payment you should also sign and return the attached statement that says you understand the terms of this agreement." Charles finished his reading.   "He wants more money right now than Eva and I get a month from our Social Security," he said.   "We'll just have to move because we don't have it."

"No, wait people!" Steve interjected as Mike muttered his agreement with Charles' assessment of their options.   "He can't do this.   I know it.   There's a phone number that the city government has been putting on TV to call if you need any kind of rent assistance.   Let me try it before you do anything.   We can't let this son-uv-a-bitch get away with this.   Let me call the number tomorrow, and I'll let you know what they say.   There's got to be something we can do."

The faces that looked at Steve were silent.   In the eyes were mirrored years of seeing humans exploiting other humans, but they were Steve's friends, and they didn't shatter his world.   They knew it would happen soon enough, anyway.

It was the morning of the twenty-third before any of the tenants saw Steve again.   When they did, they didn't have to ask.   His defeat was reflected in his stance, in the hesitation in his voice, in his chagrin at having lost the fight for them.

"We're lost," he told Charles and Eva and, later, Mike and his wife.   "You were right.   The bastard knows what he's doing.   There's no law in this state that a landlord give thirty days notice of a rent change or eviction.   I found out from the mayor's office that it's common courtesy to give such a notice, but it's not required.   And as for that help number they've been advertising on TV, that's somebody's bad joke.   All day long I tried to get through.   That's why I didn't get back with you all yesterday.   I was on the phone dialing constantly to get them to answer.   Busy, busy, busy was all I got.   Then, finally, someone answered. It's supposed to be a number that you call to get help, but you know what she said to me?   'What office do you want, sir?   All I can do is connect you with the office you want.   This is the City Hall switchboard.' When I started to tell her about Isaacs, we got disconnected.   I think she cut me off, because she seemed aggravated at being bothered.   I never could get back through again."   Steve's voice trembled with frustration, and the lump in his throat made him constantly hesitate in his speech in order to swallow. As he finished, he felt a sense of failure roll over him, and the feeling deepened as first Eva and then Charles silently turned and went back in the house.   Though uncomfortable   in   the   presence   of   Steve's embarrassment,   Mike   didn't   leave,   and   it   quickly became apparent that he had an admission of his own. He shuffled from foot to foot, eyes roaming over the backyard and up the faded walls of the deteriorating house until he found the words.

"I've got to admit something, Steve.   I hate it because you've tried so hard, but I have to tell you. The wife and I found a new place to live yesterday afternoon.   It's down on Annuciation and is almost as much as Isaacs was going to charge us here.   But it's away from him, away from this part of town.   We just had to go ahead and leave here after all that has happened, maybe find a place where we can be left

alone for a while, not bothered by this New Hope shit.
I hope you can understand."

Chapter 14

Charles, hurry up. Hurry up. If you don't come on we're going to be late for keno. You old man; you're always late." Eva backed out the door yelling as she came.

Neither rain nor sleet nor fear of sleeping on the street would keep Eva from her keno. And as the few precious days left in the month slipped by one by one, sleeping on the street became a greater and greater possibility. Charles had had no luck whatsoever in finding a new apartment, and he now stood near the open door with phone in hand, continuing to call numbers from the tattered, ink-stained newspaper that he held.

"Eva, go on to the car," he called. "I'll be there after I try one more place." Under his breath so she couldn't hear, he muttered, "you just don't understand, do you? You just don't know what's happening to us?" He turned back to the phone with a lonesome shake of his head.

Earlier in the evening he had been telling Steve about the problems he and Eva were having in finding an apartment.   He had spoken slowly, his speech ground down by the effort of the search, and his usual smile erased by fatigue.   "There's just nothing out there for what we can pay.   In three days we've only found two places that were cheap, and, gawd, what dumps they were.   One was down on Tchoupitoulas, one room and share a bath and kitchen.   The place was filthy.   It made this place look like a mansion. The other place was a little cleaner, a single room with a shared bath, but it was on the second floor, and we can't climb stairs.   We really wanted to stay close to this neighborhood, but everything around here now is at least double what we've been paying.   A black fellow with a place for rent over on Freret Street told me that all the rents have jumped up lately.   He thinks it's from all the people like us that are being kicked out so that these young fat-cats can rebuild these old houses. Poor people like us are just getting pushed further and further downtown.   I don't know what we're going to do."

"Charles, Charles.   Come on." Eva yelled from the car.

"I might as well go on to keno," Charles said to himself as he turned to obey Eva's order.   "Maybe somebody'll get in a fight at the game, and it'll take my mind off all this."

In the car, Eva was strangely quiet, occasionally stealing a glance at Charles.   After a few blocks, she slid over beside him and rode with her hand tenderly resting on his leg.

The cracked case and missing hand from Steve's alarm clock reflected his past frustrations at being disturbed from the blessed release of sleep.   On this morning the clock received a particularly hard slap as its jangling began to slowly penetrate his sleep-drugged brain.   He had just finished working twenty-four hours straight with only an occasional break.   Fatigue from the work marathon was multiplied by the emotional drain of the last few days.   He still didn't know what he was going to do about an apartment since he was leaving the city in a few months anyway.   Should he go through the hassle of moving now only to have to do it again in a short while?   Or, should he swallow his pride and pay homage to the little son-uv-a-bitch, Isaacs, for the use of his property?   There was one thing for certain that Steve had decided.   When he did move out of this place, he was going to strip it to the bare walls, taking everything that he had put into the dump over the years to try to make it livable.   He would take the sink out of the bathroom.   There had not been one when they moved in.   The heaters were his as was the gas line which connected them.   He had also added electrical wiring to the apartment, and he was going to take every box, every plug, and every screw that he had put into the place.   If his tools slipped occasionally as he worked, if a hole got knocked in the wall every once in a while, well, who was to say whose fault it was, and to hell with any deposit.

The worry over what to do, his fatigue from the long hours of work, and the fifth of bourbon that he always consumed to help him through such marathon jobs had quickly dropped him into a dreamless abyss from which he was reluctant to leave.   But the incessant

ringing of the alarm was still going on.   He slapped at
it again.   When it didn't stop, the realization finally
wormed its way into his brain it wasn't the clock at all
that was clanging away.   The sheet flew as he dove for
the phone, suddenly concerned that he wouldn't get
there in time and would never know who this was
invading his sleep.   It wasn't an intruder or an
invader.   It was Charles, and his voice came over the
line with a heaviness that shocked the cobwebs from
Steve's brain and the sleep from his eyes.

"This is Charles."   He announced himself.

Steve hesitated, suddenly dreading responding
because he knew it would be followed by the bad news
that always comes with 2:00 A.M. phone calls.
"What's up?"

"Steve, Eva's ...," Charles hesitated, "Eva broke her
hip at the keno game.   The fool woman was running
for a pot when she tripped.   They've got her down here
at the Charity Hospital, and I'm going to stay with her
tonight.   I was wondering if you would keep an eye on
the place for me until I can get home."

"Sure, sure, I'll be glad to, but is there anything else
any of us can do to help?" Steve asked.

"No, no, but thanks.   Just watch the place and I'll
tell you more as soon as I can get home.   I want to stay
around here tonight to make sure she's okay.   This old
woman hasn't been in a hospital for thirty years, so
she's a little nervous.   She won't admit it, of course.
All she's doing is raising hell with everybody who
comes around.   But I want to stay here."

"Okay.   No problem," Steve added.   "Don't worry
about the place, and call if you think of anything I can
do, anything at all."   The conversation ended, and

with a heavy heart for what Charles and Eva were going through, Steve hung up the phone.

A phone in the Isaacs' kitchen jangled loudly.   "Al, get that for me, will you?" Marc called from the next room.

"Depends," Al shouted back.   "It depends on who it is."

"Get it," Marc shot back, and Al, grinning, picked up the receiver.   It was Charles.

"Why, good morning, Mr. Isaacs.   You're just the person I was trying to get in touch with."   Charles felt a sense of relief at having finally caught up with his landlord.

"What is it now?" Al Isaacs asked, grimacing at his cousin to indicate his distaste over the turn of events.

"Well, Mr. Isaacs, uh, I've wanted to tell you how sorry I am that, uh, that, uh, Mike did what he did. I'm really sorry ...."   Charles voice trailed off in discomfort at his blatant lie and at having to shuffle for Isaacs.   Personally, he knew that pushed to the limit anyone might have done what Mike did.   He might have himself if he were younger, much younger.   He certainly had the desire.

"Yeah, well forget it.   He's gone now, anyway, and it's all over."

"Well, I'm awfully glad you feel that way, no grudges or anything, because I really need to ask you for a big favor."   Charles had trouble getting out the words.

"Well, I'm not in much of a favors-giving mood, but what is it Charles?"   Al rolled his eyes at the ceiling in answer to Marc's questioning look.

"I wonder, Mr. Isaacs, if you could see your way

clear to let Eva and me stay on at your place for another month?"   Finally, he had gotten it out.   "You see, we've been trying hard to find a place but just haven't been able to.   I'm sure we'd be able to if we just had a few more days, just a few more.   You know how it is with old folks like Eva and me.   We move pretty slow, but like the tortoise, we get there eventually."   Charles laughed nervously at his attempt at a humor that he didn't feel.

"You mean you want me to let you stay on at the same rent you've been paying?" Isaacs asked incredulously.   "No," he answered.   "No!" he repeated a little sharper, a heavy weight of weariness suddenly settling in on him at having to deal with these people who had no comprehension or concern with the financial pressures that he was facing.   All they ever thought of was themselves.   "I can't do it, Charles, and that's it."

"But Mr. Isaacs, I didn't tell you the whole story," Charles pleaded.   "Eva has been hurt.   The fool woman was running to collect a pot that she'd won when she tripped and fell and broke her hip.   She hasn't been in a hospital in thirty years, and, well, she's not taking it very well.   I've been staying with her since to try to keep her calm, and I haven't had time to look for a place to live.   If you can't give us a month, then just a few more days would help, and I would appreciate it, Mr. Isaacs."

"No, no, no," Isaacs answered tiredly.

"Please, Mr. Isaacs.   Please," Charles begged, his voice trembling.   He was close to tears as he pleaded for a little understanding.   "You don't know the whole story, Mr. Isaacs, but, you see, Eva and I aren't married.   We just live together, and she has some relatives who've never liked that.   As long as she was okay and we could take care of each other, they left us alone.   But, now that she's hurt and they think I can't do well by her, they're after us again," Charles continued.   "If I don't have us a place to live by the time she gets out of the hospital, they're going to take Eva away and put her in a nursing home.   Mr. Isaacs, I've never told anyone this but you.   I can't live without her.   I just can't do it, and I don't know what I'll do if they take her."   Charles' words came slowly now.   "I beg of you.   Please, Mr. Isaacs.   Just give us a few more days."

Al Isaacs didn't hear the last plea.   He had already hung up, tired of Charles.   He took a sip of coffee from the cup Marc handed him.

"You were kind of hard on him, weren't you?" Marc asked, having guessed what the call was about. "Maybe you should have given them a little more time. It wouldn't have hurt."

"Come off it!" Al snapped, shaking his head at his cousin.   "You can't let these people run over you like that.   They'll tell you anything.   They live by lying. And they'll find a place; don't you worry about it. Don't you either," he repeated, throwing his arm around Lori's shoulders as she walked in on the conversation.   She hadn't been very happy with Al since he had misled her about moving to the neighborhood.   She continued working with him, though, and was willing to increase her business involvement with him because of the resources he was willing to commit to the area and its cleanup.   "Keep foremost in your thinking the fact that we've got to show twice as much income from that place from now on in order to keep the bank happy.   If we double our income, I've already been guaranteed a loan to buy that next house down Camp Street, and that'll help clean up your neighborhood a little more.   You'll like that, won't you, Lori?"   He let her go as he raised his coffee cup in a toast to the two others.   "We're on our way now.   Nothing can stop us.   To the future!"

Chapter 15

Charles' exit from the apartment on the last day of March was slow and painful as he swung his bum leg awkwardly behind him, leaning onto the wall as he moved. Age pressed heavily on his shoulders, and they bowed even more than usual from carrying the additional weight of Isaacs' avarice. The exhaustion of looking for an apartment while also staying with Eva at the hospital showed in the sallowness of his complexion and in a new trembling that shook his voice as he talked.

"Steve, what are you going to do?" he asked his neighbor who was standing on the porch drinking a cup of coffee. "Have you decided?"

Steve didn't want to answer. He had put off telling Charles that he had decided to stay on for the few months until he left the city for good. He felt guilty that he had the money to make this decision when Charles and Eva did not. Somehow, it wasn't right that the people least able to make the change were the ones that were being forced to move.   So he had remained silent.   But, it was March 31st, and there was no use to hide it any longer.

"I'm staying, Charles.   I'm leaving anyway in August, and I just didn't want to move for those few months, so I'm going to pay his ridiculous rent." Steve's voice trailed off.

"Well, I guessed you were staying, Steve.   I had already guessed it."   Charles interceded mercifully, no hint of condemnation in his voice.   "But, honestly, I just don't know what Eva and I are going to do," he continued.   "I told you about what her folks want to do, didn't I?   About wanting ...?"

"Yeah, you told me," Steve interrupted.

"I didn't tell you, though, that I called Isaacs." Charles broke the silence that had followed Steve's answer.   His voice was tight as if each word were being wrung from him with difficulty.   "I asked him ....   No, I begged him ...," he halted, groping for words to express his humiliation.   "I begged him, Steve, and I've never begged anyone for anything in my life.   But I pleaded for just one more month, for just a few days, at least, for just a little time to get Eva home and then to find another place to live."

Suddenly, for the first time in the conversation, Charles looked Steve straight in the eye.   It was only for a second before his eyes dropped, but it was a look that shook Steve to the depths.   It was a glimpse into the soul of a human that has been destroyed; it was a vision of finality.   Steve hardly heard Charles' conclusion.

"He hung up on me.   Isaacs just hung up."   With those parting words, Charles inched down the steps and limped to his car.

The skies of cities are a lace of interwoven wires. Electric wires, phone wires, residential wires, business wires run helter-skelter as if the web of some monstrous spider.   One rarely sees these since city dwellers have little reason to look up.   Thus, unnoticed, the web grows thicker with the years as first one wire, then another is added, stretched, and increased in size.   This massive web is supported by a maze of poles that sprout from street corners, backyards, and fence rows: little poles and big, tall poles and short.   Remove the buildings from a city, and a forest would remain, a forest of trees, albeit without leaves, preserved forever with creosote and penta and the grafitti of passersby.   The poles support the web, but a secondary function is to protect those on sidewalks, on steps, and on front porches late in the evening from those errant drivers who stray from the streets.   In this, the forest does its job well.   On Friday and Saturday nights in our cities and towns, tow trucks and emergency crews make their rounds scraping cars and drivers from the poles where they have planted themselves.   The mutilated posts are quickly repaired and replaced to begin again their silent but protective vigil.

It was one such pole that saved the family on Camp Street from destruction on the evening of March 31st. They were simply sitting on their steps as usual, relaxing, talking, drinking.   One or two of them may have noticed the halting old man down on the next block get into his car, but they paid no attention since there were a lot of people stirring around at this time of day. They did see him, however, as one hundred feet away from them his car suddenly swung right, jumped the curb, and headed down the sidewalk directly toward where they were sitting.

"No, No, Charles!   This isn't our curb!   This isn't where we park!   This isn't where we belong!   We belong with our friends down the street at McLaughlin's place."

"Is that you, Eva?   Is that you?" Charles yelled through the fog that had enveloped him a second after a sinister jolt had suddenly ripped through his chest. "Eva!   My Eva!" his shouted reply came as a dimming thought.   "There is no McLaughlin's place.   It's Isaacs' now, and we don't belong."

The family saved by the pole set into the curb by their front porch was the first to the car.   Steve, who had seen what had happened from where he was still standing on his own porch, was second.   Other neighbors were close behind, but they were all too late. Charles was dead.

Epilogue

I leave behind the clanking old streetcar crammed with tourists and students. Swaying and popping with flashes of electricity, it has carried me away from my convention hotel and along miles of flawlessly restored mansions on St. Charles Avenue. The houses are beautiful with their ornate, beveled-glass, front doors with entry hall chandeliers, their perfectly manicured yards and gardens, and their curving walks lined with Mercedes, Jaguars, and Cadillacs. Tourists who want to see the city have been directed to the streetcars by the City of New Orleans Tourist Bureau. Happy on their vacations, they bump along not realizing that the grandeur of St. Charles Avenue is only a veneer over a very different city that exists outside the corridor.

For a long time I had wanted to simply walk through the old neighborhood. It was a ridiculous urge, I knew, since the New Hope had destroyed the area years before.   For me, that life ended when Charles was killed and Eva was taken by her relatives to end her days in a nursing home.   By the time I moved away in August, others on the block were under attack by the New Hope.   The Cranes quickly followed Charles and Eva, the house they lived in being bought by Al and Marc Isaacs.   Two months later it was the alcoholic lawyer, his wife, and the other people who lived in the building with them.   So the neighborhood was gone, but I still wanted to walk through just to see the changes that had taken place in the years since then.

So I walk, and as I do, my sense of loss and disappointment grow, making me realize that I had wanted far more than just to see the changes. Somehow, buried deeply within me, there had been some bit of hope left that there would be people on the steps, on the walks, yelling from the porches, and that I would be able to pause a few minutes with them to recapture the feeling of closeness that had permeated the neighborhood.   But no one is out.   The street with its now immaculate houses and carefully trimmed curbs is deserted.   The only sound is the constant hum of the air conditioners that New Hope families, each in its frigid cocoon, use to insulate themselves from each other.   There is no need to tarry here.   The place is foreign, peopled by strangers, and I am not a part of it.

In returning to the streetcar that will begin my journey back to my home and family a thousand miles and light years away from this place of memories, I follow a different path.   As I walk along it, I see that the invasion that captured our block years before with its horrible human consequences is still going on.

Only now, the battle front is many blocks further downtown.   As I near the line between the renovated blocks and the older neighborhoods, the houses rapidly turn to shabby multi-family tenements and the streets erupt with the sounds and smells of human existence. People are hanging from porches, talking on sidewalks, and enjoying the last bit of twilight.

Toward the end of the last block before I reenter the veneer formed by St. Charles Avenue, a feeble, old man and a slightly younger woman stand enjoying an evening conversation.   As I pause for a moment near them, they abruptly stop talking and hurriedly start into the house.   With the old man glancing nervously at me over his shoulder, the woman helps him along the sidewalk and slams the door tightly behind them. For a moment I am perplexed by their behavior, but I really shouldn't be.   In me, they see a stranger stalking in the shadows--a spy, perhaps, for the New Hope--and they, along with untold others like them, are continuing to live the story of Charles and Eva.